librev 11

D0530558

Speak easy

00095324

brilliantideas
one good idea can change your life...

Speak easy

Dazzle your audience with stunning speeches

Barry Gibbons

CAREFUL NOW...

Unaccustomed as you are...
We are enthusiastic about most things here at Infinite Ideas. For example, we think you could be a better public speaker, and think you could do more of it. To those ends, we have provided the most brilliant ideas to make you shine on the big day. You can't always open your mouth without putting your foot in it, however, and there are some risks involved. You might upset that favourite auntie of yours with an off-colour joke – and your boss just might not see the relevance of your quite legendary Jerry Lewis impersonation during your presentation to the market analysts. We have to remind you that you are all grown-up now – and while there are loads of ideas here for you, the responsibility for putting them into practice is entirely your own. We think you are potentially really cool on your feet, but we can't get toothpaste back in the tube.

There are the steps up to the stage. Don't trip now.

Copyright © The Infinite Ideas Company Limited, 2005

The right of Barry Gibbons to be identified as the author of this book has been asserted in accordance with the Copyright, Designs and Patents Act 1988.

First published in 2005 by
The Infinite Ideas Company Limited
36 St Giles
Oxford
OX1 3LD
United Kingdom
www.infideas.com

A CIP catalogue record for this book is available from the British Library.

ISBN 1-904902-16-2

Brand and product names are trademarks or registered trademarks of their respective owners.

Designed and typeset by Baseline Arts Ltd, Oxford
Printed by TJ International, Cornwall

Brilliant ideas

Brilliant features

Each chapter of this book is designed to provide you with an inspirational idea that you can read quickly and put into practice straight away.

Throughout you'll find four features that will help you to get right to the heart of the idea:

- *Here's an idea for you* Take it on board and give it a go – right here, right now. Get an idea of how well you're doing so far.

- *Try another idea* If this idea looks like a life-changer then there's no time to lose. *Try another idea* will point you straight to a related tip to enhance and expand on the first.

- *Defining idea* Words of wisdom from masters and mistresses of the art, plus some interesting hangers-on.

- *How did it go?* If at first you do succeed, try to hide your amazement. If, on the other hand, you don't, then this is where you'll find a Q and A that highlights common problems and how to get over them.

Introduction

Armed with one of the few diesel-powered laptops left on earth, I am writing this in a hotel next to a convention centre, in the heart of a major US city. In about an hour, assuming I can find my cufflinks, I will go on stage and give the fifth of five speeches to an audience of about five hundred management employees of a global US–Japanese corporation. The first of the five speeches was about four weeks ago. Each convention has been in a different city, but with exactly the same format. I go on last each time, and I get as near as I can to repeating myself, which is sometimes not very near.

Two things have made themselves clear to me. First: I have confirmed my view that the standard of public speaking in a frightening percentage of senior management in both the UK and US world of business (where you might expect trained professionalism) is crap. There are some good, and some exceptionally good, but it's generally bad. Second: if you want to improve, you can. Rapidly. I base this last thesis on watching the company's Big Cheese through all four of the previous events. I had no choice – he was on before me, and introduced me. He then had no choice but to watch me. His first performance was like an 'I speak your weight' machine. His second surprised me: he stole a lot of my gestures and mannerisms. His third surprised me even more – he stole two of my best lines.

These two observations of mine are the genesis of this work.

Speaking in front of an audience does not come easily, or naturally, to most people. That's a bit of a problem in modern life because not only do a lot of people want to be able to do it, a lot actually need to be able do it on a regular basis. Family occasions appear quite regularly on the radar screen these days, and the trend is for them to be bigger and more formal. Sometimes you have an unavoidable responsibility to speak – but how many of us, without formal duties, envy the ability of someone to stand up and 'effortlessly' blend a bit of humour, articulation and emotion in a way that makes everybody feel good? Your sports or social club is forever trying to put together events – and the hunt is permanently on for someone to help the evening along, even in a subordinate role to a professional after-dinner speaker. Wouldn't it be something to steal the show?

In business, or organisations of any kind, the need to address an audience and convince them of something is becoming a core competence. Small businesses are not excluded. It's no good making the perfect jam if you can't stand in front of the retailer's buying team and convince them to put it on their shelves, or present a credible business plan to potential investors. On the lower slopes of big business, teams are often presenting the results of project work, ideas have to be sold to senior management and 'management' briefings are now quite significant events as technology continues to remove layers of management. On the higher slopes, quite regularly there is a need to address large audiences, via a variety of media, in a convincing and motivating way.

Finally, if you look in your telephone directory, you will be surprised at the number of speakers' agencies listed. Yes, you can get paid for it, and I do. There were two reasons why I didn't get angry at my Big Cheese for nicking my style and content. First, his company paid me handsomely. Second: I actually stole both from somebody else – or, rather, a bunch of 'somebody elses'. The point you want to note is that there is a big market out there for professional speakers – which is just like show business in that you don't have to start at the top of the bill.

It was my Big Cheese friend who got me typing the first words of this work. Sure, few people are naturally good at public speaking – but, if you want to, and/or if you need to, you can learn and improve ridiculously quickly. In his case, it took fifty minutes of watching me and he damned near turned his sow's ear into a silk purse. This is not about fanning my ego (remember, I got there via many fifty-minute sessions watching others); it's about how fast you can dramatically improve your style, content and (above all) your confidence.

These 52 ideas cover everything I know, and some things I didn't, which I had to look up. They weave together twelve years of experience in front of audiences ranging in size from 10 people to 15,000. I've used every media, and been in every format. If it's possible to make a mistake, I've made it, or seen it made – and, more important, remembered what was done to fix it.

Whether your goal is money, career development or impressing your auntie, I will guarantee you something that may surprise you. Allow for a few stumbles and then you will start to get it right. When you get it right you will realise something that never occurred to you before. It is that these weird folk who can stand up before an audience, and who can hold them or entertain them or convince them or motivate them – and sometimes all of the above – actually enjoy it.

That's what still drives me. As for you – there's nothing to fear and nothing to stop you.

Good luck.

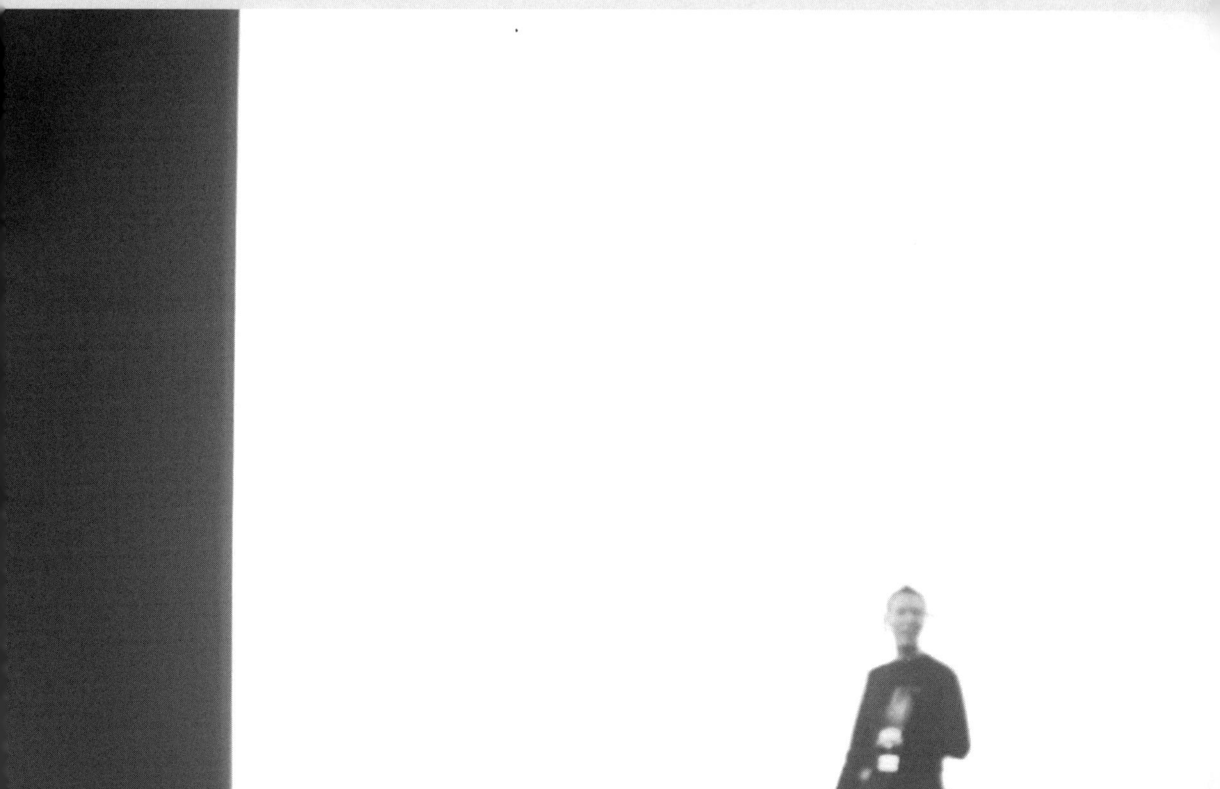

1

Just say no

It's natural to think that, if you are developing yourself – or your career – as a speaker, every opportunity is 'right'. But some gigs are just not worth it.

In your aim to turn speaking into a more rewarding part of your life there's a temptation to say 'yes' to every offer. At worst, surely, you will get low risk practise in handling a crappy audience or badly managed event?

Learn to judge each offer on the full facts and to say no to the wrong ones. There are three broad reasons why a speaking opportunity may be wrong for you.

GETTING OFF YOUR CONTENT STRENGTH

If you are a retired soccer player, working the speaking circuit because your pension went on losing horses, then you can ignore this. Your speech content is to explain to drunken audiences that you knew (intimately) a couple of stars who occupied the lower slopes of celebrity – and that one put it about a bit and the other was a drunken prat. For the rest of us, it's not so easy. If you have a general area of expertise you will be vulnerable to the conference organiser who wants specialisation. For example, if you have had successful experience in business

Here's an idea for you...

Let me introduce something called the CIA factor. The letters stand for Confusion from Implied Assumptions, and it is the cause of about 90% of things going wrong on the planet, including Iraq. It is usually evidenced by one party saying to another, 'Oh, I thought you meant...' Make yourself a list now of the factors you want clarifying before you commit to a speech. Make sure they are all ticked off before you ink a deal or shake a hand.

management, and talk generally on 'Leadership', of course you could and should adapt your content to the audience and the event. But you should not accept an offer to speak on 'Penetrating Difficult International Markets' in front of an audience that lives in that world. You have nothing to gain and a lot to lose.

LOGISTICS

I'm giving advice here as one who has accumulated much scar tissue from getting this wrong. Committing yourself to a speech before you know the full logistic implications is just as daft as being pulled off and away from your content strength. You might suddenly get a call from somebody's executive assistant to the effect that the 'briefing chat' you assumed would be a twenty-minute phone call is, in fact, to take place in the office of the executive responsible for the event. This office is 300 miles away. The executive in question can fit you in at 7.45 a.m. next Tuesday. That's a whole day lost – unplanned and unpaid. In addition, the actual time of the speech (and sometimes the venue) frequently gets changed as the final details get nailed down, and you might find yourself suddenly having to stay the night before, or after, or both. The message is simple: nail all this stuff down before you commit – or

The key to making sure it's the speech for you is in the briefing: try IDEA 4, *Brief Encounters.*

Try another idea…

you might find yourself involved in an exercise riddled with what the accountants beautifully call 'negative value added'. And that might not just be about money. Get all the material elements in writing.

DOWN A SNAKE

The speaking market or 'circuit' has an effective and efficient jungle telegraph. It is linked by people such as those who work for production companies, or those nominated in companies to organise conferences. If you get it wrong, it will get known. Trust me.

'A speech is a solemn responsibility. The man who makes a bad thirty-minute speech wastes only a half hour of his own time. But he wastes one hundred hours of the audience's time – more than four days – which should be a hanging offence.'
JENKIN LLOYD JONES, US writer

Defining idea…

How did
it go?

Q   I made an honest mistake recently and misjudged my audience. I'd done my research as well as I could, but – for whatever reason – I was suddenly at the event, due up to speak and it was patently evident that they were gearing up to hear something I couldn't deliver. What followed wasn't pretty. Should I have pressed the 'abort' button?

A   *There are two rules to follow if you get caught like this. First: do not bluff. It's not a good scenario you've found yourself in, but you are not holed below the water line. One way to sink your ship, however, is to try and be an expert in something in which you are not. Stay within your areas of knowledge and competence. Second rule: find some common link, however tenuous. I sold hamburgers. If I was suddenly confronted by a gaggle of real estate executives, as happened last week, then the common thread was that we all had customers. I built my speech around what I had done and seen done over the years in winning and retaining customers, and emphasised that I knew it would be alien to their science. But I suggested that many of the successful principles could be transferred.*

Q   I found an extra trip to a company headquarters had been inserted in my 'assumed' schedule for an unplanned briefing – which effectively took me a day. I didn't want to lose the gig, so I went along with it. Fully costed, I probably lost money on the whole thing. Should I have refused to go?

A   *Don't acquiesce quietly. Make it quite clear you agreed a set of assumptions that did not include an unplanned and unpaid day. Make it clear it's a deal-breaker. Most senior executives spend their lives dealing with other parties who are tough and have an agenda. Make your point honestly and be prepared to lose the gig. It's likely you will win the day and your stock may well rise.*

2

Ask not what your clients can do for you

It's an early – and potentially grave – mistake to forget that you need to impress the person who hired you, not just your audience.

From the moment you agree to give a speech your mind becomes focused on how you will impress the audience-in-waiting.

But there are two audiences you should seek to impress. The obvious one is the audience at the event. The other one is the person who has booked you on their behalf. This person is your customer. It is almost certain that your customer will have a different set of success criteria, identified for the event, from that of the actual audience.

Who are these people – these customers of yours? They range from the social secretary of the sports club to big-budget, highly professional event-production executives. Included in that wide range are people such as communications directors, PR managers, HR executives and the chairman's personal assistant. All of them are likely to have three things in common:

■ The success of the whole event, which may not just revolve around your contribution (however difficult you find that to believe), will reflect on them. If they score an own goal they can adversely affect their positions and/or careers and/or businesses.

Here's an
idea for
you... **If you have to have an AV
presentation coming up,
finalise it now and then don't
change it or let anyone near it. I
have seen many presentations
wrecked – and many customers
driven batty – by speakers
wanting constant changes
and/or making basic mistakes
with the technology. I once saw
a brewery manager briefing
trade union officials on the new
three-pronged forklift trucks he
was proposing to introduce.
They would cut labour, so it was
all very tense. His cause was
not helped by the pictures of
the new trucks appearing on
the screen the wrong way up.**

- They can affect your ability to succeed on the day.
- They may hold the key to other, future, speaking invitations that could head your way. It is to these people that other potential clients might come for references or recommendations.

Here are four ideas whereby you can help your clients make sure the whole event reflects well on them.

- From your very first conversations, let it be known that you understand the importance of time (and timing) to the success of the event. Nothing – absolutely nothing – penetrates the lower bowel of a conference organiser further than a speaker who believes the whole event is about him or her, and that he or she has a licence to ramble on for an hour and a half after having agreed a forty-minute slot. So, stress that you understand that. More than that, indicate that you are the kind of speaker who can help if things go wrong elsewhere – for example being flexible enough to pad out or cut short if the timetable starts to disintegrate for whatever reason.

- Recognise and anticipate your customer's constraints. These are often budgetary, so once you have agreed a fee (if there is one) enter into the spirit of the event. If it's tight, don't flounce about demanding helicopters and hotel suites. Volunteer to jump in a cab, or to travel home to avoid an overnight hotel stop. The fee is the important thing, and it is fair game to exhaust their budget getting what you can here – but you will score a big number of points with the organisers if you don't play the Hollywood Diva after that. The constraints might be technical – most places can provide the wherewithal for a slide presentation, but not that many can accommodate an audio-visual show. If that's the case, don't insist. Find another way to get your message across.

Have a look at IDEA 30, *You can look at me or look at that*, if you are uncomfortable working with AV technology

Try another idea...

- Make it clear that you have a backup travel plan. Don't get the last possible train or plane. When you arrive at the location, contact the client direct. The hours before most meetings are chaotic, and it will be genuinely appreciated if you take the time and effort to let them know that at least one part of the proceedings (i.e. you) is on track.

*'The customer's always right, my boys, the customer's always right.
The son of a bitch is probably rich, so smile with all your might.'*
NOEL COWARD

Defining idea...

- If you have an audio/visual presentation, don't keep changing the bloody thing. The good news about modern AV software is that you can change your slides right up to the last minute. The bad news is exactly the same. From your customer's point of view, few things will induce more nervous tension than any speaker who is still tapping away at the keys of a laptop while their walkie-talkie echoes with the crackling message that the doors are opening in two minutes.

How did it go?

Q   **I arrived at an event, and only then realised that my client – the person who booked me and 'organised' it all, was a complete plonker. I worked doubly hard to help and we all got through it. The trouble was, I made him look good when he wasn't. Should I have left him to cock it all up?**

A   *This happens more than you would believe possible, and you did exactly the right thing. There is no guarantee your efforts will a) save the event and b) help your current and future cause. But it might, and if it doesn't you will get your reward in heaven. Remember this: if you leave it all to go tits-up, you might suffer more than anybody.*

Q   **I finished an event where everything seemed successful. My customer seemed very happy. It seems sad to just finish abruptly like that. How can you keep the buzz going and benefit from it?**

A   *After every speech, write to, or email your customer – the client who booked you. Simply thank them for the invitation, reflect your view that all seemed to go well and your hopes that the total event succeeded in its goals. This will keep you top-of-mind if they are approached for references or recommendations. If they respond, chances are you will get some nice words to add to your endorsement library.*

3

Anyone here from outta town?

Audiences are not the same. Every one is different. They have different needs and wants.

Good speakers celebrate that fact, not fear it.

I knew a professional speaker who was short-sighted. He told me that, if he took his glasses off and got the lighting turned down a bit, then all audiences looked the same. He thought this was a brilliant way to conquer stage fright and concentrate on his material. He failed as a speaker.

I got wind of this difference in audiences way before I ever considered speaking as a profession. I worked for a brewery, and was taking the chairmanship of a 'Ladies Auxiliary' (a gaggle of publicans' wives doing charity work). The outgoing chairman, a sales manager for a sherry brand, gave an after-dinner speech to which I was to reply. To my horror, he told a filthy joke in an appalling Australian accent. When I dared to open my eyes, all I could see was an array of fruit bobbing up and down. It was the hats. The women were all laughing, uncontrollably, with their heads down. Afterwards the guy told me that you cannot embarrass an all-women audience. If it's all men, sometimes you can also go 'deep blue'; if it's mixed, never, never

Here's an idea for you...

Define now the three or four 'commonalities' that might link your normal audiences. For each one, define some key goal(s) of your speech relating to those common factors. Then refer to these as you write each speech. You will find yourself authoring quite different speeches. If you are struggling to find out anything about your upcoming audience, take a short cut. Ring up last year's speaker and ask.

venture beyond the palest blue. I have no idea why or how that works, but it does.

That's a Neanderthal starting point, but I didn't invent humanity. I know it might seem obvious, but you must find out what you can about the basic demographics of your audience and use common sense. If it's made up of twenty-somethings, don't rely on anecdotes about Winston Churchill. The more subtle tricks are to make judgements about the audience's commonality, and the event's climate.

COMMONALITY

Let's say you are invited to speak at an event hosted by a big corporation. The idiot speaker turns up and delivers a one-size-fits-all speech. The good speaker realises that a single corporate host might be hosting any one of a range of audiences that want and/or need a different kind of speech. Here are two examples:

■ The audience might all be direct employees – an 'internal' company meeting. You are not going to be able to make yourself aware of the intricacies of internal politics, but the simple fact is that there will be bosses and subordinates in the same room. Check first, and you can probably poke a bit of gentle fun at the bosses. But be wary: this kind of audience is not free-range. There are inhibitions and barriers about that need respecting by a speaker.

■ The audience might be all customers of the host company – in which case they are likely to be representing businesses themselves. They might have nothing in common other than the fact they buy something like accounting software from the host company – and might themselves be retailers, manufacturers, distributors, high-tech, low-tech, public sector, private sector (etc., etc., ad infinitum). They might seem to have nothing in common – but if you hunt you will find something. It might be as simple as the fact that they, themselves, have customers, or that they are small businesses, or have common economic or market problems. They might even have a common enemy. Find some commonality and use it.

For more thoughts on what you can and can't get away with, check out IDEA 15, *A funny thing happened on the way to the crematorium.*

Try another idea...

CLIMATE

Let's turn now to the importance of the climate of the event when you are figuring out how to work your audience. Take a 'barometer' reading with what information you can get. Then set yourself a goal: improve it or maintain it – but don't worsen it.

'If all the world's a stage and all the men and women merely players, where do all the audiences come from?'
DENNIS NORDEN, UK television personality

Defining idea...

The climate might be obviously bad. That might be down to poor market conditions, poor business performance, lay-offs, pestilence, famine, weather, sports' results – whatever. This is not a good time for anything silly. Respect the seriousness. Abandon levity. However, you are not being paid to add to gloom – so work in some optimism.

'It's as well to try and find out.'
BARRY GIBBONS

...and another...

If the climate's good, and it's celebrations all round, hey, go for it. Try that Billy Connolly routine you've been practising in front of the mirror. If you can't do it here, you'll never do it. He won't mind.

13

How did it go?

Q **I was briefed to speak at a business convention – but it was only when I got on stage that I realised that they'd invited spouses and children in to the general session. I ploughed on with my speech, but it was tough. Should I have tried to make changes for the wider audience?**

A *Yes. Not many, but some. A good idea is to limit changes to the opening and closing. It's fairly easy to adapt both for this broader audience – and will let you deliver your main messages as planned.*

Q **When I got up to speak, the house lights went down. I couldn't see a face. I felt I lost contact with my audience. It threw me, and my performance suffered. How do you get a 'rapport' with darkness?**

A *Think of four people who like you – or would like you if only they had the chance (in my case that would include Halle Berry). Position them, in your mind, in four different places out there in the dark. Then talk to them alternately.*

Brief encounters

If you fail to prepare, you should be prepared to fail...

By far the best route to effective preparation is to get an exhaustive briefing.

If your speaking 'market' is the male-oriented rugby/cricket/golf club after-dinner circuit where the objectives, in no particular order of priority are: a) for everybody to get rat-arsed; b) for event revenues to exceed costs thereby funding the purchase of new balls and c) to hear behind-the-scenes tittle-tattle about some C-list sports celebrities, you, as a speaker, will not feel the need for a pre-speech briefing. For the rest of us, my message could not be clearer.

Take advice from the best. I booked the UK comedian Bob Monkhouse for a corporate event some years back. It's difficult to know with Bob when he was actually at his peak, as he was at it for so long, but he was up there at the time. He arrived early. I was the MD of the host company. He wanted a briefing and he wanted it with none other than me; our briefing chat lasted – seriously – two or three times longer than his eventual (brilliant) speech.

Many event hosts will insist on briefing you – they rightly see it to be in their interests. If they don't, you should invoke the Monkhouse Rule and insist on it. Either way, try and get into conversation with somebody who owns responsibility for the event.

Here's an idea for you...

If you've got an imminent booking, find out now if the event will have any formal feedback: questionnaires, session marking forms, whatever. Request a copy beforehand. If you know how you will be judged, it will help you shape your content and style.

All events involve the expenditure of some costs – time, money, deflection. If you spend, you should seek a return. Here's a good place to start: what 'return' are they looking for from the event generally, and your bit specifically? Have they identified any success criteria? Are they measurable? It is perfectly sound to host an event with the loosey-goosey goal of having fun as a reward for success – but the trick is saying so beforehand. Whatever the goal of the event is, it is important you know it. Then, you can shape your approach.

In establishing the goal of the event, don't be confused by some strap-line or 'theme' for it which is splashed about everywhere. This will be probably be couched in corporate bollock-speak (for example, 'The Way Ahead', 'The New Tomorrow', etc., etc.). Ignore that and see if you can get an articulation of what they really want out of it, and you. Such a goal has to be one, or a mixture, of the following:

- Reward/celebration for some good news
- To inspire/motivate to greater things
- To sell – an idea, a programme (which might be good news or bad news), a product or a service.
- To educate/brief/inform

If it's a big industry multi-day convention, it may attempt all of the above – but it's likely the real goal will be limited to one or two. If you can nail that (or them) down, it provides an essential background for you to shape the appropriate content and style of your speech.

You can get a quick and dirty briefing by sitting in the audience for the session before yours: see IDEA 6, *Sitting in the back row.*

Try another idea…

Let me sound a couple of warnings around the briefing process. Firstly, the danger of overbriefing. This is not giving you too much information – that's impossible. This is about some jobsworth trying to write your speech for you. A good briefing gives you the context to do that yourself, which is how you want it. Overbriefing, with too much detail, and too many 'It would be helpful if you could make reference to our exciting plans to outsource our call centres to India' kind of directives can not only lose you a lot of spontaneity but end up with your client failing to get what they are paying for – i.e. you.

Vincent: 'I'm gonna take a piss.'
Mia: 'That's a little bit more information than I needed, Vince, but go right ahead.'
QUENTIN TARANTINO, *Pulp Fiction*

Defining idea…

Secondly, beware becoming a bearer of bad news. A couple of times, after 'thorough' briefings, I have realised I have been set up either to break the news or set the scene for some upcoming doomsday stuff. When you see that coming, stomp on it.

'That works for Vince peeing, Mia, but for speech briefings you can't have too much information.'
BARRY GIBBONS

…and another…

17

How did it go?

Q   **I tried, but I just could not get near the 'event responsibility owner' for a briefing. Do you just fly blind on these occasions, with no idea what they really want?**

A   *No. Never mind for them, this isn't good enough for you. It is in everybody's interests that you become bloody-minded here. The first stage is simply to ask more questions and take more time. If you are still stuck with the idiot minion, then formally ask them to ask somebody else. If that fails, find out who the responsibility owner is, and write to, or email them directly. Tell them you are booked to speak, and that you'd like your input to be in line with the goals for the event. That'll work.*

Q   **I was struggling for a briefing prior to a speech. Does it make sense to get stuff from the host organisation's website if you are short of a good briefing?**

A   *For a while I thought this was a brilliant source, but I've now stopped looking at them. A website provides public-domain information for a specific set of purposes, but an event is about a time, place, audience and zeitgeist which may bear little or no relation to them. Find out about the event as a one-off.*

5

It's all in the timing

You will find different parts of the day – and programme positions – suit you and your material best.

Recognise the different needs of a speech and speaker at different times of the day, or at different points on the programme.

Morning speeches have an entirely different DNA than after-dinner ones. Personally, there is only one time I dislike: after dinner. It shows in my performance, so I avoid it when I can – even if it means giving up lots of folding stuff. I know some speakers love it, but for me these speeches always start (very) much later than planned and I end up cutting my time and reeling off a few jokes just to escape.

At the other end of the spectrum, the programme position I love is any time during the day at a business meeting where I follow a consultant, armed with eighty slides, who overruns for twenty minutes. I like it because the audience love me before they see me or hear me.

Make your mind up about the best timing or position for your style and content. Summarise it, in crayon, on the back of a business card. Then, if you are asked, you have it handy. If you are not asked, make sure they know anyway.

To help you make your mind, here are some of the variables in play.

Here's an idea for you...

Make a note of this: a US marketing guru I know has a great technique for opening an end-of-session spot. He bounds on stage and directs his audience to stand up and 'wiggle your asses'. It never fails.

'GRAVEYARD' SESSIONS

There are two: the first morning session if there has been a 'heavy' night before, and the first afternoon session. With the latter, a long morning is behind, a long afternoon looks to be ahead, lunch is lying on the tummy and the contents of seven lunchtime phone calls are deflecting the mind. It is not just that energy is low, people are actually resistant. The UK comedian Ken Dodd tells of a particularly tough, northern club audience. He had given his best – and got nothing back from them. It was only afterwards, mingling with the crowd, where he got an inkling of the forces at work when he heard a man say to his wife, 'Eeeeh. That Ken Dodd were good. I nearly 'ad to laff'. Think of Ken Dodd's audience when you face a graveyard session. You need to compensate for their low energy with your high energy, and you need a great opening to overcome their resistance.

If it's a morning session, after a rough night before, then let your audience know you understand how they feel – and get them on your side. Here's one I've used to break the ice. Morph your introduction into the fact that you arrived late and checked in while it was all still flowing. Say you were interrupted at the hotel check-in by a couple of delegates, demanding a 6.30 a.m. alarm call. The guy on reception told them it couldn't be done. This brought on a rant from one delegate about poor service and inadequate technology. He was just getting into his stride when the reception clerk stopped him: 'Sir. It's 6.45 a.m. already. Go to bed'.

Defining Idea...

'The head cannot take in more than the seat can endure.'
WINSTON CHURCHILL

EVENT OPENINGS AND CLOSINGS

These are honoured slots. You will be instrumental in setting the tone for the events ahead, or crystallising a lot of minds as they turn their thoughts to home. Respect this honour – and make sure you are thoroughly briefed. If it's a closing, this may mean getting some last minute input into how the event you are actually attending has gone.

END OF SESSION SPOTS

These are the last in a series of presentations. These spots are usually just before lunch or breaking for the evening. I love these (see my comments about the Dutch consultant above). Your enemy is sensory fatigue, so go for simplified content and powerful delivery. A good rule is to avoid slides of any kind. A golden rule is not to overrun.

If you are stuck with a boozy after-dinner gig, look at IDEA 26, *Ish a pleasure (hic) to be here.*

Try another idea…

'There is but one pleasure in life equal to that of being called on to make an after-dinner speech, and that is not being called on to make one.'
CHARLES DUDLEY WARNER, US editor and author

Defining idea…

'So when's best for you, Charles?'
BARRY GIBBONS

…and another…

How did it go?

Q **I was booked for the opening session of a big conference. When the official start time arrived, virtually nobody had taken their seats. It took the best part of twenty-five minutes to get them in and ready. I was only booked for a forty-minute speech, so I had to cut and made a mess of it. Should I have overrun?**

A *Yes. You didn't have to cut. Most conferences start late – and the experienced organisers plan for it and build some slack into the programme. Unless you are specifically asked to cut, just stay calm and carry on as though nothing had happened. It's OK to overrun here – but not in the final session.*

Q **I was on last in the morning. The sessions ran late and the organisers asked if they could serve a plated lunch during my speech. I agreed, but it was chaotic and I lost my audience. What could I have done differently?**

A *You can digest a meal, or you can digest a presentation. You cannot do both, and you should fight like hell not to be the speaker faced with such circumstances. In your case, the organisers had problems, so you shouldn't just add to them. See if you could help with a solution. This might be starting the afternoon session early, or cutting a bit from your speech, or doing without the afternoon break. Maybe a combination of all of them. But be strong – avoid the lunching audience.*

6

Sitting in the back row

All the research and briefing in the world will not provide you with the real thing. Experiencing other speeches from the audience's perspective can give you some great pointers.

If you have the opportunity, get to the venue early and sit in on the preceding session (or sessions). Do this anonymously, if you can. It is pure gold.

By 'sitting in' I do not mean joining the audience for lunch or a tea/coffee break. I mean sitting in the audience while the preceding presenter(s) do their thing. Yes, you are stealing; you are a plagiarist – not of material, but of the experience.

Your God, hopefully, gave you two eyes. Sit at the back. Train one eye on the speaker and the other on the audience – so that you can witness how they are responding. What are you looking for?

Well, firstly, you are studying the speaker. You are looking for things that go well with this audience – and things that don't. I guarantee you will change at least two things in your planned content and/or style if you witness one previous speaker – changes that will result in a win for you and for the audience. Here are some things to pick up on:

Here's an idea for you... **If you can sit in the session before yours, identify three or four receptive minds and/or friendly faces. When you are up on stage, search them out – and start your speech by talking to them again.**

■ A couple of useful reference points. It may be an 'internal' company speaker, who will come up with a couple of key figures, or some collective goals that you can refer back to ('As Harry just pointed out, you've got a 10% earnings growth figure right in your gunsights.'). An external speaker might light up a couple of verbal sparklers that are worth repeating and reprising.

■ A statement of the obvious – but I'm making it. Watch out for microphones that splutter or have limited range or slide screens that can't be read from the back. Sometimes, you can turn it to your advantage. I pre-sat a speech at an event where the sound systems were so cocked-up that we (the speakers) ended up with three lavalier microphone systems wired underneath our suit jackets. I looked like a well-dressed Mancunian suicide bomber. I opened my speech by walking to the front of the stage looking miserable, muttering the words, 'You've no idea how difficult it was getting through Dallas airport like this.' I was home and hosed.

■ Pick up the obvious style and content lessons. If the speaker swears, and the audience freeze, don't do your Lenny Bruce impersonation. If the speaker's a Johnny-one-note and it doesn't go down well, start mentally practising an extended vocal and movement range. I once followed John Major, the ex-UK Prime Minister, at some big corporate knees-up in Hawaii. The only reason I went on after him is because he had a plane to catch, so I got star billing (honest). John is a lovely man, and his content was interesting. His delivery, however, looked and sounded like a plank of wood. He lost the audience early on, and never got them back. I went on and performed a cross between a cattle auctioneer and a windmill. Cheers all round.

Next, listen to the audience around you. If you can do it without being obvious, watch as well. You will find that the back seats of any decent-sized auditorium, which is reasonably full and reasonably dark, have their own ecosystem (this should come as no surprise to anybody who has survived their teenage years).

If you can't join the audience at least try and get into the room before your speech – see IDEA 8, *The feng-shui factor.*

Try another idea...

They are always the first seats to fill up. Sometimes, particularly in the US, some folk like to stand at the back – and if it's a big event there is likely to be a steady trickle of standing up, sitting down, coming in and going out. You will have the noisiest, most responsive folk there – and you will have those who don't want to know you (the speaker) or the event. The cynics will congregate there, and attempt to breed cynicism. In short, it's full of real-time stuff you want to know about and can never research. This is where you will get the truest read on the 'climate' of an event. Many is the time I have found this quite distant from the official briefing position – and the experience helped me to make some important sensitivity adjustments before I went on.

'Plagiarise... Remember why the good Lord made your eyes...'
TOM LEHRER, US musician and satirist

Defining idea...

How did it go?

Q **I sat in at the back of the audience for the speaker before me – and it wrecked my confidence. They were groaning and moaning amongst themselves and just taking the mickey out of the speakers. Shouldn't I just abandon this idea?**

A *If you would rather not know this, you will need a Plan B for your career. For one thing, as soon as they see you on stage, they will twig that you have been quietly sitting amongst them for a while, which will shut some of them up. For the rest – target them. If they are near enough, make eye contact. Use some humour, maybe use a couple of snippets you picked up. There's a good chance you can turn this to your advantage.*

Q **I watched the speaker before me. He was brilliant and got a standing ovation, which shattered my confidence. Wouldn't I have been better not knowing about his success?**

A *Steal from the best at this – the UK comedy writer and speaker Barry Cryer. He treats everybody who precedes him as a show-stopper, and starts by praising co-speakers (like me), while diminishing himself. He then proceeds to make a speech that makes us look like amateurs. If there are good vibes from the previous speaker, let it boost your confidence.*

7

Sermons and snippets

**The length of your speech is likely to be determined for you
– at least, that's what the organisers think at the outset.**

But sometimes you can change it, and
sometimes you might have to change it –
so it is as well to know your own best time span.

The optimal length of a speech is a function of timing and content. Finding out the
right mix for you is another key to successful speaking. Find out what it is, and be
ready to fight to get it or to defend it.

A good discipline is to aim for slightly less stand-up time than you think you really
need. As the Americans say: a recipe for a good speech always includes shortening.
On the other hand, a stupid – and possibly mortal – mistake is to assume you need
more than you actually do.

How important is timing? It is vital – and not just from the point of view of your
performance. I have done hundreds of speeches, and they invariably have a
common element. Prior to the day of the event, most of the discussions and
briefings are about content. On the day, however, the priority always becomes time.
On one memorable occasion, at a chaotic event with massive presentation overruns
and the prospect of a post-midnight finish, the organisers asked me if I would
accept an increased fee for a decreased speech length. Too bloody right I would.

Here's an idea for you...

Without going into all the detail, structure your material into two speech lengths. Make the longer one your 'preferred' speech, but have a shorter one structured and ready to substitute if circumstances need it.

The optimal timing for any speech and speaker is unique. My personal view is that the vast majority of substantive speeches can be encompassed within a time envelope of between twenty minutes (the absolute minimum) and fifty minutes (the practical maximum). Below that insults everybody – unless it is to deliver a specific content (e.g. to introduce somebody, or to thank the Academy for your Oscar). Beyond fifty minutes, the audience can get numb bums, and you risk rambling and/or getting lost.

A key determinant of your optimal timing will be whether the content is information-based, or anecdotal. Both these should be entertaining, or you are not doing your job. If your speech is information-based it is likely to be at the longer end of the time spectrum. You might be selling a product or a service, or briefing an audience on some upcoming programme or event. It might be motivational, showing how you conquered Everest, or scored tries for the national rugby team. Essentially, however, it provides information – often data-based and frequently visual – and that needs time to be digested if it is to be effective. If you quite genuinely can't get the data across and digested in less than fifty minutes, break the session into two. All will benefit.

The anecdotal speech is different. The speaker is saying: 'This is me. These are my reflections and experiences, and I'm making them relevant for you.' These kind of speakers are often pre-Copernicus (i.e. they think they are the centre of the universe, and should therefore have a licence to rabbit on for hours), but I've seen very few who can't get the job done in thirty to forty minutes.

If you are struggling to get your speech time down, look up IDEA 22, *It's a wrap.*

Try another idea...

Don't be afraid to propose a change to your planned time on the actual day. Unless you arrive at the last minute, you will soon become aware of how the event is going. Many organisers fly these things by the seat of their pants, and value input from an experienced speaker. Here are a couple of examples that worked for me:

■ I was booked to do a complex evening event – involving an opening, pre-dinner, thirty-minute speech, then to have one course of my dinner on each of the three tables (of ten people), then to finish the night with a five-minute summary. You couldn't make it up, could you? As it happened, it was pouring down in Birmingham that evening, and we barely filled two tables. The organiser was embarrassed and increasingly panicky. I 'suggested' we abandoned one table, got straight into dinner, served the coffee with the dessert, and I would do a straight forty- to forty-five-minute, humour-led speech. I nearly got a hug – the organiser being a woman.

■ If you are booked for fifty minutes, but are genuinely of the view that the state of the event, audience and timing is such that they could do with no more than thirty minutes, then ditch your ego and propose exactly that to the organiser. Make it clear you are happy – and prepared – to do the longer time, so the option is completely down to them. If you've judged the state of the event right, it will be much appreciated.

'Hubert, a speech does not have to be eternal to be immortal.'
MURIEL HUMPHREY (to her husband, then US Vice President)

Defining idea...

31

How did it go?

Q I am so aware of the importance of timing. How can you keep a check without constantly looking at your watch?

A *You need to identify three key 'timing' milestones in your speech content. When you reach them, then – and only then – check your watch. The elapsed time in relation to where you are in your content will tell you if you have to speed up or slow down – or cut or pad it out.*

Q I use quite a few slides – which different audiences digest differently. Some ask no questions, some get bogged down with them. How can I manage my time with this difference?

A *Do not allow questions during a speech. You are instantly out of control, and risk losing everything. Make it clear at the start, if there's a lot of data or they want to follow up on something, that you will take questions afterwards – either in open session or on a one-to-one basis.*

8

The feng-shui factor

You probably won't be able to choose the venue for your speech. However, if you put your mind to it, you can affect most of the other variables affecting it.

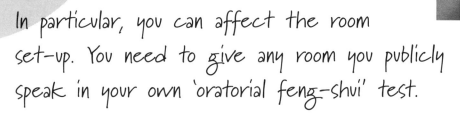

In particular, you can affect the room set-up. You need to give any room you publicly speak in your own 'oratorial feng-shui' test.

All speakers have personal preferences here, and the ability to make a few small changes can have a big impact on your confidence and success. The organisers will be concerned with a lot of cosmetic stuff, making sure the room looks good. You need to make sure that the beauty is combined with practicality – which will enable your speech in your style to be delivered and received effectively.

THINGS TO CONSIDER

- Will your audience be able to see and hear your speech? The golden rule when you arrive at a venue is to assume nothing. Check it out. Sight lines are more likely to be a problem than hearing ability – and it may well be that you have to move about a bit more, or a bit less, to give visual access to everybody.

Here's an idea for you...

It's tough enough winning the audience over on your own; you do not need other people or things up there competing with you. I have arrived at many venues to see the stage setting including half a dozen seats for the organising committee or the elder statesmen of the conference – and found, to my alarm, that they planned to sit up there while I performed. This is a deal-breaker for me, and should be for you. Ask them, politely, to vacate the stage while you are on. If they are not happy, then you should – calmly – assemble all your toys and throw them out of your pram.

- Check where you come on from, and go off to. About 90% of organisers haven't given this a moment's thought, but your opening and closing are two big impact points for you. Try not to be in view while you are being introduced – but if that's not possible make sure you have fast, clear access to the speaking point. Going arse over tit at this stage is not helpful. Similarly, at the end of the speech make sure somebody will pick up the microphone after suitable (extensive!) applause. Standing there while the applause embarrassingly dies away does not leave the audience with a positive image of you.

- Check the house lights. Rooms are usually set up with the lights on (or in daylight). It can throw a speaker if they have been part of this, and then are suddenly faced with a dark auditorium. Check what's planned for the lights – and you will find they will probably ask you what you want. I like it light enough to pick out friendly faces.

- Take responsibility for placing your 'stuff'. Do not delegate any of this – place your water, notes, props, visual-aid switches (etc., etc.,) exactly where you want them.

- Each to their own here, but my preference is to combine my speaking position with the audience layout in a way that enables me to be as near as possible to as many people as possible. If you are speaking from a fixed point, that means arranging the seats in front of you, half of them on either side, and just out of spitting distance (in case you get carried away). Don't plan to get closer than that. If you are a 'free-range' speaker, you need to check your sound and visual range, and then organise your paths so that you can nearly spit on as many of the audience as possible.

If you are not sure about standing at a lectern or moving about, try IDEA 18, Moving target. It looks at the pros and cons of both.

Try another idea…

You will need to work out and add your own personal preferences to these, so you can quickly decide on – and implement – any changes if you should get any (usually brief) pre-speech opportunity. Here's a personal example: like it or not, a lot of speaking occasions involve meals. If I get the chance in advance I will try and organise the room set-up so that I can leave the meal table and give the speech from a more central spot, where I can also move around a bit. Here's my thinking: if audience members have knives, I need to be able to move about.

'We should learn from the snail: It has devised a home that is both exquisite and functional.'
FRANK LLOYD WRIGHT

Defining idea…

How did it go?

Q **I gave a speech in front of a good, receptive audience of 150 people – but the problem was that they had booked a 600-seat room for the event and the audience was scattered all over it. What can you do to 'herd' people towards the front?**

A   *This is a classic feng-shui opportunity. If you get to the venue, and become aware of the 150 and 600 figures, then you have an opportunity to make a real difference to the event. Ask the organisers to block off the back 450 seats, using a couple of marshals or signs or tape – or all three.*

Q **I turned up at a venue, and found I was to give my speech 'in the round' – with the audience all around me. What can you do to avoid half the audience looking at your bum for forty-five minutes?**

A   *Basic rule – you cannot give a speech to an audience in the round from a fixed podium. You have to fully face each ninety-degree segment of the audience for a quarter of your time in total. That (to me) means ditching the lectern as an anchor point, using minimal notes and/or visual aids, and lots of movement. I like these set-ups, and they are becoming more and more popular – so be prepared.*

9

Life with lecterns

There are only two alternative speaking 'positions' – fixed and flexible.

You can either be tied down or roam freely...

A fixed position means you are anchored to something (like a table, a microphone stand or a lectern), and thus severely restricted in your movement. The flexible speaking position has no restrictions of substance associated with any of the above.

A lectern is the most common anchor. Do not be drawn into using one just because it is there. Learn to hate it, and avoid it where possible. Follow my habit and request in advance that there be no lectern. It is the speaker's equivalent of the wooden horse of Troy. It looks nice and it looks unthreatening. In reality, it is an enemy.

Why are they such a no-no?
■ They cause dead hands. Men, particularly, don't know what to do with their hands when speaking; hence the fact that if they ever put pocket billiards in the Olympics, Britain's male speakers will own the gold medal spot. With that in mind, watch a male speaker the next time you see one behind a lectern. Where do his hands go? Within a nanosecond, they grip each side of the lectern. And they never move again. At a stroke, the speaker loses one of the best weapons in his armoury for effective speaking – the gesture.

Here's an idea for you...

I don't get any money for this, but buy a copy of Ricky Gervais's *Animals* DVD. He's the UK comic who created *The Office*. It's (rude) stand-up comedy – but (unusually) he uses a lectern. It's a great example of using it as a space station and to create intimacy, whereby it's used sparingly to great effect.

- Lecterns encourage reading. However much you've rehearsed, if you dump your notes on a lectern, the temptation is to start (at best) referring to them, or (at worst) reading them. There are occasions when it is right to read aloud in public, but those occasions are not here and they are not now. Your eyes need to be looking in front of you, at the audience. You need to find faces you can relate to, and you need to constantly watch the audience for signs and signals that give you feedback as to how your speech is going. Most speakers get their essential speaking nutrients from audience feedback, and you will miss out by spending large chunks of time peering downwards.

All that lectern-hating is fine, of course, but the reality is that most speaking venues come with one provided – and most speakers (including me) need somewhere to dump their 'stuff' – backup notes, small props, water, etc. In which case, use it – but use it for that purpose and that purpose only.

Think of a provided lectern as a space station: float about the stage, doing your thing – then pop back to the station now and again to do something specific. Spacemen, of course, would use it to pee, eat and sleep. You can use it for a variety of things. Perhaps you need to lighten proceedings up? Pause, and drift back to the lectern. Slowly sip your water. All eyes (trust me) will be on you. When you've had your (slow) sip, say: 'You all think this is water, don't you? Ha! This is an old trick taught to me by the late Queen Mother...' Use a trip to your 'station' to bridge different sections of your speech, or use it to consolidate if you are spinning your wheels a bit.

You can use it specifically – and cleverly – to create intimacy and impact. In 1996 President Clinton was being challenged by Bob Dole for the US Presidency. They were in a televised head-to-head debate, answering audience questions. It was all very, very structured, and they were both positioned behind lecterns. Both had two minutes to reply to the same question. Up it came, and Dole batted first. He had obviously rehearsed, and he got all his sound bites in and was very professional – albeit a little cold. Same question to Clinton. He said nothing, but walked from behind his lectern to the front of the audience, looked the questioner right in the eyes and started his answer with the guy's name. Game, set, match: presidency.

If you want to explore the idea of using fewer or no notes at all, try IDEA 23, *I'm sorry, I'll read that again.*

Try another idea...

'Rex (Warner) doesn't believe in using lecterns; he sees them as a barrier between you and the audience. He says: "What are you afraid of? Walk round, get close to the audience. If you're worried about forgetting your speech, carry your notes round with you".'
MITCH MURRAY, citing REX WARNER (explorer and speaker) in his *Handbook for the Terrified Speaker*

Defining idea...

How did it go?

Q **I was set up to use a radio lavalier microphone (a 'tie' mic) at a recent speech – and it failed at the last minute. I had to use the lectern microphone, and was stuck behind the bloody thing for my whole speech. How can you 'liven' up a speech if you have to use a lectern microphone?**

A *If this happens, take your time and check exactly what the lectern microphone can and can't cover. Everybody will know there's a balls-up, so don't rush. What you will find is that the lectern microphone can probably pick up from the side well enough, so – at worst – you can stand by the side of the lectern and remove the 'barrier'.*

Q **I am nervous at the start of a speech, and find a lectern helpful as it stops my hands shaking. Once I'm through that, I'm all right. Isn't a lectern useful for this at least?**

A *No problem. That's a good use for a lectern, as long as you knowingly limit it to that. A lectern can have a number of positive uses – but not as a direct speaking aid.*

10

Testing ... testing

Progress in communications technology over the last generation or so has not missed microphones and sound systems.

They are potentially more effective and efficient than ever...

As a speaker you are an assembly of the key direct variables which will affect the success of your speech – your looks, your sound, your movement, your messages. Beyond that, there is no single accessory that has a bigger impact on your performance than your microphone and sound system.

The audience can't usually see the sound systems that deliver the sound from the microphone into the auditorium, but all can see the microphone. There are three main types:

- Hand-held (think about Tom Jones).
- Fixed position – either on a stand or attached to a lectern.
- The lavalier – attached to your clothing somewhere. These come in two parts – the microphone bit, which is usually a tiny attachment that will clip to a collar or tie, or up around your neck somewhere, and a small, (usually) Walkman-sized attachment which you need to hide.

Here's an idea for you...

If you use a lavalier microphone, when you've tested it leave it switched on at your box, and get the sound man to lower your channel sound at the mixer and then bring it up as you go on. That means you don't have to touch anything – but be warned: this is not then a good time to go for a pee.

Whatever you choose, the normal optimum position for a microphone is about 20 cm from your mouth, and it should keep that distance as constantly as possible during your speech. Now, you may feel you have to go with the microphone that's provided, but it is so important that I advise you to make your preference known beforehand.

Here's the first question to ask in determining your preferences: do you actually need one for the particular occasion? Most organisers will provide one, but it is surprising how many times you would be better off without one. If you are close to them, using a microphone to an audience of fifty or less is overkill. If the acoustics are good and you can get among them, you could probably add half as many again before you have to wire up.

If you need one, my advice is to choose or lobby for a system that keeps both your hands free. Even if you prefer standing still (in fact, even more so if you stand still) you need your arms and hands to gesture. Apart from gesturing to support your words, you might be juggling an array of spectacles, a water glass, notes, visual-aid switches, props and so on. On top of that, your ability to keep a hand-held microphone at a constant 20 cm from your mouth is, frankly, nil.

For me, a lavalier works best. The downside is that the 'Walkman' pack needs hiding, and they do vary in size from a pack of cards to a shoe box. The good news is that the latter are getting rarer, and they can now usually fit into your back pocket or clip to your belt or waistband under your jacket. It's a problem for women if they do not wear some jacket/pocket/belt combination, but the women speakers I know still prefer the lavalier for the mobility benefits.

If you are worried about 'occupying' your hands if you are not holding a microphone, look at IDEA 17, *Give yourself a hand.*

Try another idea...

Whatever you use, don't trust it. Few microphone and sound-system combinations are actually designed specifically for the room they are in at the time – so test them personally before you go on. If that means getting there at the previous break, and having to then wait for your session, so be it. You may have the advantage of a 'sound man' if it's a big event, but whether you are accompanied or solo you must test for two aspects of range:

- Range of movement. If you move about with a lavalier, or a hand-held microphone, at some stage it is likely you will cross an invisible line and cause a shriek of microphone feedback that would alert walruses on heat in the Arctic. Find that line before the speech, and memorise or mark it.
- Range of voice. Set the sound level for your normal delivery voice, but remember you will raise your voice for the dramatic bits, so test those as well.

When you've tested it, set it and don't let anybody touch it till you get on.

'Some microphones work great as long as you blow into them. So you stand there like an idiot blowing and saying "Are we on? Can you hear me?". It's only when you speak the microphone goes dead.'
ERMA BOMBECK

Defining idea...

'Modern microphones are small and high-tech. Like anything else that is small and high-tech, they should be trusted as far as you can throw Canada.'
BARRY GIBBONS

...and another...

How did it go?

Q **I was promised a lavalier microphone, but when I got to the venue it had a wire running from it to a backstage unit. All was going well until I forgot about the wire and did a horizontal bungy jump. The audience were happy for all the wrong reasons. What could I have done?**

A *These are horrid things, and now all but extinct. If you do get one pushed towards you then seriously explore doing the speech without any microphone or treat it as a fixed one – that is, don't move. If you do, the wire will get you.*

Q **When I worked with a lavalier microphone last, it was clipped on my tie and kept brushing against my jacket lapel making a noise which confused everybody. Any tips on avoiding this?**

A: *If you clip it to your tie, you need to check it is free of potential 'obstacles'. If you have a jacket on, fasten it. If the microphone's still likely to brush against the lapel, then clip it to the lapel itself. Keep it clear of obstacles and interference (like loose change in your pocket).*

11

Speaker flies undone

The audience expects you to be dressed as a figure of authority, whatever your subject.

If that's not important enough for you, consider this: the audience will draw conclusions from your appearance that can make or break your speech.

I am a serial scruff-bag. When I'm travelling to a speech, I often get given small change at transport termini. When I arrive at a location, if I'm getting an advance 'feel' for the stage, or doing a soundcheck, I look like I've been dragged through a hedge backwards. When I start my speech, however – no matter wherever and whatever the venue or circumstances – all of the above is gone. I will be suited up, and accessorised with collar, tie, shiny shoes and cufflinks. I can't really advise women speakers on dress – apart from the absolute basic principles, which apply to anyone.

Here's the first one: from the moment they see you, the audience will begin making its mind up about you. There may be just thirty seconds from that first sighting until you open your mouth – but it may be much more if you've been in sight

When you travel to a venue, with your speaking outfit either already on, or in a carrier ready to change into, carry an emergency repair kit with you. Obviously, if somebody upends the claret jug over you there is not much you can do – but you can handle the odd tear or lost button easily these days. A bit of tape and emergency 'stick-on' buttons are essential speaker's accessories. In addition, I always carry a tiny backup pair of off-the-shelf reading glasses, and an emergency tooth-crown repair kit. One more piece of travel-related clothes advice: if you are flying to your venue, take your speaking clothes with you on the plane as hand luggage.

during a lengthy introduction or have sat through a previous session or meal. Whatever that length of time is, all the audience will have to work on is your visual appearance, your 'image'. You will not score many positive marks in this examination for appearing neat and tidy, but you will be heavily marked down for appearing the opposite. Dirty, unkempt hair is a big no-no, but after that things like missing buttons, shoddy and crumpled (and outdated) clothes, 'lumpy' pockets, one pocket flap in/one pocket flap out, stained ties and dirty shoes all work against you – and this is before you've opened your mouth.

Your invitation to speak might include a dress code – 'business attire', 'smart casual' or even 'business casual'. Ignore all such daft language, and dress formally, even if you use informality as an element of your style and content. For one thing, it removes the problem of choosing what to wear, and – frankly – it means you can't go wrong with one important variable in your performance.

If you're not a suit person – and I'm cautiously suggesting that this might be a good idea for women as well – I'd still go with a jacket of some kind. You can carry a number of things with you, even in a tight-fitting jacket, without risking the 'lumpy pocket' effect. In a normal speech, my jacket will hide the lavalier microphone wiring, and the battery pack which is hooked on to my trouser belt just at the back of my hip. My glasses are in my top pocket. My 'notes' are on a single small envelope, which is in my (left) inside pocket – where they normally stay, unused. And that's it. In fact, with the suits I use just for speaking, I have left the jacket side pockets sewn up – so as not to be tempted!

Ooops! Sorry! I forgot – I also carry my lucky charm. Strangely, a lot of speakers I have come across are superstitious – a bit like sports players. If they have a good win (or a good speech) they like to repeat the formula, or carry a lucky mascot of some kind. I wear a small (Irish) lapel pin which does the job for me, and my only advice on this whole lucky charm subject is to echo Bob Monkhouse: carry around what you want, but don't rely on it to the extent that, if you are about to go on stage and suddenly realise you haven't got it with you, it works in the opposite direction, having a negative effect on your ability to deliver.

A lot of venues now have a video facility – and will show a simultaneous screen show of you speaking, and may produce a video after the event. So, wear a dark suit – which takes off about 1.5 of the 4.5 kg (3 of the 10 lb) video normally adds to your weight.

If you're not sure how to work with minimal notes, look at IDEA 23, *I'm sorry, I'll read that again.*

Try another idea...

'*Clothes maketh the man.*'
MARK TWAIN

Defining idea...

'*We all know what dishevelled is. Don't go on stage until you've checked in a mirror that you look shevelled.*'
BARRY GIBBONS

...and another...

How did it go?

Q **At a recent business meeting, the audience were away from their normal place of work and all very casually dressed. I felt like an alien in my suit, and my performance suffered. Should I have met them half way and dressed down?**

A *Emphatically not. Remember their expectations of you as a speaker. If it is palpably obvious that you are the only guy in the place dressed formally, then you can use that fact to break the ice a bit. Have a bit of fun with yourself in the opening – for example: 'As I look out I see two hundred people. That's two hundred minds with but one thought – where did he get that tie?'*

Q **If it's summer, and/or the air conditioning doesn't work, and/or they leave the heating on, and you are sweating and uncomfortable, surely you can take your jacket off?**

A *I wouldn't – but you can make a joke about it ('I'm sure you've noticed I'm sweating a bit – all I would ask is that those who are also sweating do not raise their hands...').*

12

And with us tonight...

There is one key variable affecting 'lift-off' that most speakers assume is beyond their control or influence – which is their introduction by a third party.

They tend to just grin and bear it — or, rather, in many cases I have witnessed, wince and bear it. You don't have to.

Speakers are wrong to delegate the content of their own introduction to a third party. It is true that the speaker cannot control the style of an introducer, but he or she must control the content.

It's a nightmare. You've done everything you can to get yourself and the set-up right, and then whoever's been given the job of introducing you stands up before a microphone. Anything can happen next. What you want is a short, informative, flattering introduction – pitched in a way which will complement the style and content of your speech. I could fill a book with pen-portraits of what you often get:

- The Ramblers: who go on and on and on because they have never had a microphone and a big audience before.
- The Terrifieds: who amazingly combine five indecipherable grunts with three inaudible whispers.

Here's an idea for you...

Sometimes you will get the job of introducing other speakers. It may be that, after you have finished, you need to link to the next part of the programme – or it might just be that you are there so somebody asks you to do it. Here's the rule: do unto others as you would have done to yourself. No rambling, terrified grunting, administrating or comedy. Play it straight, and err on the side of flattery. Next time, they might be introducing you...

- The Administrators: who take advantage of the microphone and audience to run through essential housekeeping instructions such as – true story – advising an audience that the brewery who had sponsored the evening in its function room was requesting that members of the audience would kindly not piss in the car park on the way out...
- The Comedians, who decide to weave into their introduction of you about fourteen appallingly told jokes.

The solution to this is in your hands. Step in and take control.

There is one simple way to do this. Write down your preferred introduction, and send it to the organisers in advance. Write it in at least 18 point font size, so it can be read by somebody on their feet, in front of a microphone, in a (possibly) darkened room and who is also feeling nervous. Politely request that this is the introduction you prefer, and that it is important that the introducer does not stray from it as there are a couple of points that you link to at the start of your speech. Most organisers and/or 'delegated introducers on the night' will welcome this – in fact the more enlightened ones will ask you for it.

Let's assume they agree – happily – to stick with your script. What do you put in it? Is it a time for modesty, or do you blow your own horn? Can you flick a few jokes in, or should this be serious with the fun coming in the speech itself? Should it be long and informative, or a brutally short summary of your triumphs?

Look at IDEA 3, *Anyone here from outta town?*, on ways to analyse an audience so you can match it up with your most appropriate introduction.

Try another idea...

The answer is: all of the above. You should have several versions, each of a different 'personality' and length. You can then make a judgement about the audience, the event and the location – and pick the most appropriate one. I would suggest, however, that all of them fall within a time range of between twenty seconds and a minute. When you've chosen it, send it in advance. When you've sent it in advance, print it and take a spare copy with you – they are bound to have lost the original. In fact, I carry spare copies of 'all' my introductions – sometimes I change my mind when I've got a closer feel for the event.

Remember, introductions are sales aids. They are supporting the sale of you as a product to the audience – who are potential buyers. If you want to be modest, that's fine – but only do so if you believe that modesty will help your selling cause with this particular buying audience. I cannot overstress this: do not write your intro to make yourself feel good. Write it to make a specific audience want to listen to you. I like to add a teaspoon of self-depreciation and mix a bit of fun into mine – even with the shortest: 'Our speaker tonight, Barry Gibbons, is the only person to appear on the front cover of *Fortune* magazine sporting a mullet hairstyle.' The *Fortune* bit impresses everybody, then they cheer up with the fact that I'm a sad bastard as well.

Control, n. Power of directing, command; restraint; means of restraint, check.
Oxford English Dictionary

Defining idea...

Q **I briefed an introducer with what I thought was relevant information about me for this audience. He missed some key points out. Should I have mentioned them, or does that make me sound big-headed?**

A *If it's important to the 'selling' job, get it in. You can tint it with a smile and a bit of self-deprecation, but if it's important that the audience register it, weave it into your opening.*

Q **I've just followed the world's worst Rambler who introduced me. He went on for ten minutes and – frankly – lost me the audience. Should I have interrupted him?**

A *No. It's unlikely to be practical or polite to interrupt – and a bad way for you to start. You do need to get the audience back with you, and you can do that by having a carefully benign bit of fun at the Rambler's expense: 'Of all the introductions I have ever had ... [pause five seconds] ... that was certainly one of them.'*

13

Another opening, another show

The opening of your speech is the equivalent of a mountaineer establishing a base camp.

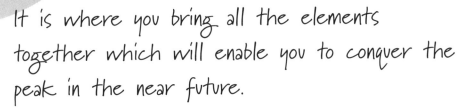

It is where you bring all the elements together which will enable you to conquer the peak in the near future.

There are about a thousand books on public speaking. The majority of these books contain an idea that they have plagiarised in common – the old adage that you should 'tell 'em what you are going to say, say it and then tell 'em what you said'. The first bit should not be confused with the opening of the speech.

Remember, the base camp is a critically important phase in the success of an expedition, but not the one it will be remembered for. The clever mountaineer makes sure that all the important technical, practical and mental variables that will be needed for the ascent are all present and in working order. In the same way, the clever speech maker checks out and sets up four things:

■ Everything is working. The microphone is the obvious one, but the opening is where you also check out the lighting, what you can and can't see, where you

Train your breathing. To get your pacing right – and your voice projection, timbre and rhythm – you need to breathe correctly. If you do, you will find that the pacing nightmare goes away, and the thing almost becomes natural. Most people breathe from the upper chest region, with short shallow breaths. The key is to breathe from the diaphragm. Here's how you find out where this is (!), and test whether you are doing it properly. Put the back of your hands, fingers pointing backwards, on each of your lowest ribs. Breathe in through your nose, feeling your ribs expand as your diaphragm does. Go as far as possible. Then reverse it, breathing out through your mouth. Do this a few times before you go on stage. If there is a sound from your throat as you exhale, you are tense – so repeat until it's silent.

can and can't move, that your AV stuff and (any) props are to hand along with your water glass – an essential accessory for many things other than just thirst. If something's not right, stop now and fix it.

■ The opening is not about key content. The reality is that, although the audience will be able to hear you, their digesting process is slow to begin. They will need a bit of time to get used to your image – and then your voice. So don't open with the key message, or a clever one-liner. I don't use my opening to 'tell 'em what I am going to say'. It's time for one or two anecdotes or narratives – maybe a minute each – which will bridge from your introduction to the beginning of your speech structure.

■ Prime the audience. The anecdotes should be chosen carefully to get the audience in the right frame of mind to receive your speech. At the end of the opening they should be picking up things and wanting more. My goals are to get my audience physically settled, relaxed, smiling and intrigued.

■ Your own pacing. It is vital that you get your pacing right during the opening. All speakers suffer from nerves. The most common way for this to manifest itself is for you to start speaking like a machine gun. This is one reason why a couple of mini-

If you want some thoughts about the kind of content that might be suitable for opening anecdotes, look at IDEA 37, Unaccustomed as I am.

Try another idea…

narratives or anecdotes are ideal at this stage – they give you a vehicle to establish your pacing. You need to include one or two, three to five second pauses – which seem like ages to you but are nothing to your audience. Move about, loosen up, move your voice up and down, but stay s-l-o-w.

Achieving these four objectives actually impacts on the audience. It is not an explosive impact, and it is not the same impact that you hope your key messages will achieve later in the speech. It is more subtle than that, but no less powerful. It is an impact which is the result of you soliciting sympathy from the audience and, at the same time, signalling that you are not to be trifled with. I call it the Aunt Dahlia syndrome, she of Jeeves and Bertie Wooster fame. She was a diminutive, vulnerable old lady who exuded a persona that unfailingly froze Bertie to the spot. If you pull these things off in your opening, you are up and running.

'There came from without the hoofbeats of a galloping relative, and Aunt Dahlia whizzed in.'
P. G. WODEHOUSE, *The Code of the Woosters*

Defining idea…

How did it go?

Q **I find opening a speech difficult as there seems to be an increasing behavioural trend for audience members to arrive late, and disturb everybody (including me) while taking their seats. Is it best to just ignore these folk, or make some comments?**

A *This is part and parcel of the opening. At best you will probably get one latecomer, at worst (particularly in the US) you may get a sizeable portion of the audience proving how cool and clever they are by arriving late. Don't be thrown by it, but if it is more than two or three simply pause and make the polite point that you will wait until everybody is settled. Do not be insulting or rude – if you make enemies of these people the audience will side with them.*

Q **Almost every time I begin a speech, you can guarantee that somebody's mobile phone will go off. Should you ask for them to be switched off before you start?**

A *That's not your job – but you might remind the introducer or organiser to make an announcement. If it still happens, I would be more 'aggressive' in dealing with it than I would a latecomer. Most audiences get annoyed by this as well – so a very pointed remark from you ('I think your chicken's ready,') will work in your favour and make sure everybody else checks their phones are switched off.*

14

One step at a time

It's time to talk about the structure of your speech content.

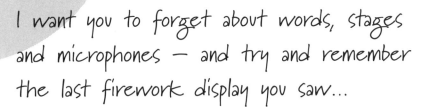
I want you to forget about words, stages and microphones — and try and remember the last firework display you saw...

Your speech needs to be structured like a firework display. Amongst the continuous energy, noise, visual impact and entertainment there will be a few memorable individual fireworks. A speech audience is only capable of remembering a few things – so structure it like the firework display. Make it all good, but ensure you have some points with real impact, and don't have too many of those.

The big mistake in pre-planning a speech structure is to overstuff it with key messages. Any audience's propensity to remember is very limited – and you can prove this quite easily by trying to remember the content of a performance that you have recently really enjoyed. I doubt you will remember more than three things.

With this in mind, a good place to start your pre-planning is to identify three to five elements that you really want the audience to remember. Lay these out in front of you like five metaphorical paving stones, and then start to infill around them.

Here's an idea for you...

Pick one key phrase out of your speech material – and work on your structure so that you can repeat it at least four times. Some time ago, Martin Luther King made a memorable speech, and I bet you can remember its title. Go on, have a go. There you are – you're right: 'I Had a Dream'. Except that it wasn't called that. That's what we remember from the content. And we remember it because he repeated it nine times in the single speech.

Let's assume your opening phase is over – so now it's time to 'tell 'em what you are going to say'. In my book this stage is less than 10% of the speech time, and asks rather than answers questions. Let's assume, for example, that one of your 'paving stones' is the following: 'Companies are now getting distinction in the market place in a different way. It used to be based on what they did. Now it's based much more on how they do what they do. The leader's role has therefore changed irrevocably – from being an expert at doing things to personifying what the business stands for.' That's only fifty-odd words, and might sound like a succinct lead-in – but it's still too much information for this stage. The audience will start running ahead of you. This is better: 'It is my contention that leadership in business has changed irrevocably – and I'll be telling you why I think that – and what I think the implications are.' That will get them intrigued and waiting.

When you get into the heart of your speech, you already have your paving stones in place. Obviously, you can't just say three things in a speech, and each point will have subordinate elements, and/or supporting anecdotes or evidence. These will be triggered in your mind when you arrive at the key point, and you must remember to get back to that base when you've dealt with them. You also need to decide how you will give each key point optimum impact – and that may be through a theatrical gesture, or by a powerful impact line, or an effective visual aid or simply by playing on the audience's emotions (humour, amazement, shock, etc). Whatever 'tactics' you use, two things must happen:

Another way to emphasise a key point is to use your hands: look at IDEA 17, *Give yourself a hand.*

Try another idea...

- The key points are finite. The audience must be clear that something important has been said, and that something different lies ahead. It's time for the speaker's pause, or the drink of water, or the change of stage position – or all three. If it's critically important, stress it with brief repetition or a mini-summary.
- Key points still need to be a part of a whole. It may be that your speech title offers a common theme, or the key points may be in a progression of some kind. Use your linking words to (gently) remind the audience of what it's all about or why you are moving from this paving stone to another in the sequence.

When you are ready to leave your last paving stone, it's time to summarise (tell 'em what you've said). This is also less than 10% of the speech time, but whereas the 'tell 'em what you are going to say' stage simply asked questions to intrigue the audience, you have now made your speech and you should have answered them. The summary, in brutally short form, emphasises your answers and proposition(s).

'Speeches are like steer horns – a point here, a point there and a lot of bull in between.'
From an editorial in *Liberty* magazine

Defining idea...

61

How did
it go?

Q **My speeches are really presentations – built around the sharing of a lot of information. There aren't really any 'key' points – just lots of lesser-but-equal ones. How can you structure that to make it memorable?**

A *I have never seen a speech or presentation that could not have been structured (or restructured) along the 'paving stone' model. There are always a few points that are worthy of emphasis, and you can relegate most of the other stuff – for example briefly summarise it, or dab it about in the infill material. Better still, put it in a handout afterwards – in that way the audience will get a fair chance to digest it.*

Q **When I pre-plan a speech, I end up with notes and ideas all over the place. How do you prioritise to a handful of key points?**

A *Rank them. But that ranking is not just about perceiving how important the 'message' is in isolation, it needs to factor in how you can deliver and support it – and the mood, expectations and make up of the audience. Sometimes style wins out over substance. That's show business.*

15

A funny thing happened on the way to the crematorium

Most speakers look back on their own speeches with a critical eye, but if you are good at your game, the audience will not have noticed most of your bloopers.

There is, however, another category of error that can have devastating effects in the way an audience receives your speech...

If you make even the smallest blunder in an area of sensitivity that is common to some or all of the audience (a 'no-go' area), even if it's an honest mistake made as a result of simply not knowing the issues involved, it is likely to be a mortal, self-inflicted wound. If you have any doubts about a potential no-go area, keep your mouth closed on the subject.

I have been in audiences where I have witnessed speakers hit a no-go area head-on. Everybody in the room is immediately aware that something has changed – it is as though an invisible Mexican wave goes through the audience. In putting down some ideas on avoiding these bear traps, I am not dealing here with the seemingly obvious ones of religion, politics and swearing/slang. These are not obvious no-gos, anyway, but here are some thoughts on minimising the risk of you getting caught.

Here's an idea for you…

If you have a speech coming up, check any references you plan to make about individuals. Here are my two rules: first, do not do this unless you are well briefed by somebody who is responsible for the event and, second, still don't include it unless you have seen that person, alive and kicking, at the event. There is no 'no-go hit' worse than rabbiting on about some poor person who was fired or taken ill that morning.

- The first is the obvious one. I ask the organiser(s) – and anybody else I can contact who might have useful input – to tell me straight if there are any no-gos. If they say there aren't any at all, I ask again, just to make sure. These things can be a mystery to you as an outsider, but that doesn't make them blunder-proof. They can be quite subtle – if, for example, you have a business for an industry-wide association, you will have competitors present in the same room. That's fine, as long as you don't allude to them benefiting by colluding while they are together.

- Don't let the organisers get you to be the bearer of bad news. If you are going well in a speech, and then you weave in the information – briefed to you beforehand – that the North West Region will be closing at the end of the year, you will die. That's not what you are there for.

- I was appointed CEO of a world wide company based in the US. I worked hard on my first speech. I thought I would throw a bit of humour in to de-tense the climate. I had long been a fan of Peter Cook's rather odd-ball 'English' comedy, and stole one of his lines from his letters to *Private Eye*, where he used to pose as a doddery old retired Colonel. He used to refer to his dear lady wife 'whose name temporarily escapes me'. My wife was on the top table with me as I stole the line. She laughed. Nobody else did. I was reported to my own HR department for sexism. It changed my whole approach to speaking. Today 'political correctness' is a major factor to consider in any speech. Let me debunk two myths: this is not just about the US, nor is it OK to be incorrect when the brandy flows after dinner. Most of it, frankly, is just common courtesy. But here's the good news: it should not inhibit a good speaker or dilute a good speech. You have plenty to work with without resorting to offence. Take it from one who had to change. It's here, so live with it.

Want to deal with religion or politics? Check out IDEA 40, 'As God once said, and I think quite rightly...'

Try another idea...

- There is a lot of public-domain information available today – and you can use it in preparing your speech. Done correctly it can strengthen your credibility – but it can be dangerous. If you want to try one or more of the Three 'C's in your speech (Cutting, Clever or Current) then do not rely solely on public-domain information for your sources – particularly the internet. The Three 'C's are risky – but effective if done well. To be effective, however, they rely on your source information being spot-on, which usually means having insider knowledge. If you haven't got access to it, they are no-gos.

'A closed mouth gathers no feet.'
BILL COLE, US poet

Defining idea...

How did it go?

Q **I have agreed to give a speech shortly, and had my briefing session. The organiser has seen a demo tape of a similar speech of mine – and has asked me specifically not to use a particular section that he thinks will be received negatively by his audience. I disagree and as I think it's a highlight of my speech, I don't want to leave it out. Should I fight my corner?**

A *No. In the case of no-gos, the customer's always right. Going against a client briefing can lose you a lot of future speeches. Word gets around.*

Q **In a recent speech I had one of those 'oh no!' moments when I realised I had inadvertently hit a no-go right on the button. I carried on, but it wasn't pretty. Should I have stopped and apologised and cleared the air?**

A *No. You did the right thing. As Shakespeare said (or he should have done): 'You can't get the toothpaste back in the tube'. To try would simply ensure that this is what your speech would be remembered for. Carry on regardless, give it your best shot, retrieve what you can and learn your lesson.*

16

Laugh? I thought I'd never start

Whatever the main purpose of your speech (sharing information and/or motivating and/or selling something) you have a single additional responsibility: to entertain.

If you want your audience to remember even a few key points, the flat delivery of content, even supported by visual aids, will not get the job done.

As a speaker you must entertain. So, unless you can sing and/or dance, and/or do card tricks and/or do somersaults it is likely that humour will be the most effective way of making your speech memorable. You can provide your own evidence to support this. Go back to your school days, and I will bet you that there is a high correlation between the subjects in which you did well and the teachers you liked. I will then bet you that there is a further correlation between the teachers you liked, and those who – even occasionally – made you laugh.

So, humour it is. Handled correctly, it is a marvellously effective resource (weapon?) to turn the water of dry content into the wine of a memorable speech. But it's the

67

Here's an idea for you...

For your next speech, stick a spouse or a close friend in the audience – and ask them to report back on two things: what went down the best, and what got the worst audience reception. Don't argue (you are the worst judge in some cases) – ditch the former, and bring in a new one off the bench. Take the one which went down best and polish it. It's a jewel.

'handled correctly' bit that's tricky, because if you get it wrong you are leaving the audience with dry content delivered badly. Here are some dos and don'ts that have worked for me.

- Do not tell the audience, in advance, that you and/or your content will be funny. People make their own minds up about comedy, and one sure way of getting them to decide that something isn't funny is to tell them when to laugh and at what. But the opposite works well – if it comes as a surprise, it comes as a really pleasant one.

- Humour as delivered by speakers has changed in my lifetime. This change has been led by professional comedians, but has implications for all speakers. It is not just about 'content' (e.g. the use of cruder language or the advent of political correctness); it is about the move from punchlines and 'jokes' to 'observational comedy'. The big names of today (Eddie Izzard, Jerry Seinfeld, Billy Connolly, etc.) fill a show without a punchline in sight. They talk anecdotally about life around them – and the humour comes from a combination of exaggerating the (abundant) daft stuff and supremely professional delivery. The implications are positive for today's public speaker. On the one hand, one-liners and punchlines are notoriously difficult to deliver if you are not a pro, and even more difficult to link to your content without sounding artificial ('I'm going to talk today about new ideas on customer service, and I am reminded about the Englishman, Irishman and Scotsman crossing the Sahara in a balloon...'). It is much easier to find stories and anecdotes which are both funny and support your proposition – and they are easier to deliver. If you can't think of any, watch the DVDs of those comics listed above and nick one or two.

A lot of humour delivery is about confidence. For some ideas about boosting yours, look at IDEA 28, *You're so vain*.

Try another idea…

- When using humour, consider any no-go areas, and don't personalise your targets. There are obvious common figures of fun everywhere – railways, airports, you name it – but the safest target of all is you. A measured dose of humorous self-deprecation goes down well with almost every audience. I used this daft anecdote recently at a speech in London – and it brings together a number of the points I'm making: 'I'm delighted to be back in London. I find audiences here are so attentive. Recently I was asked to do a book reading and signing at a breakfast business meeting at one of the big bookstores. On these occasions, the store provides coffee and croissants and the author gets to sign and sell a few books. We had a good turnout, and it was only when I paused for dramatic effect – while reading my chosen extract – to establish eye contact with my audience, that I realised I was facing about fifty of London's homeless.' It's actually true, it's funny, it's relevant to the location, it's not hard to deliver, it beefs me up a bit (author, book signing, blah, blah, blah) but shows I'll take a joke at my own expense. It also comes as a surprise.

- Keep your stuff fresh. I don't care how good the stories are, your overall performance suffers if you get stale. It keeps you on your toes if you try at least one new idea each time out.

'I can trick you into learning with a laugh.'
SIR W. S. GILBERT

Defining idea…

How did it go?

Q **I shared a two-speech spot with a professional comedian recently, and my funny bits suffered in comparison. Should I have just cut them out and not tried to compete?**

A *No. Audiences are not stupid, and they will judge the professional comedian on a different set of criteria. Think about complementing, not conflicting. Give it your best shot – then sit back and enjoy the comedy.*

Q **I gave a speech to an audience for whom English is a second language. It was all hard work, but my jokes were met with damn-near silence. Should I have tried more 'local' jokes?**

A *No way. If it's where I'm thinking, that can only be called kamikaze behaviour. Go the other way. These are unique occasions and need different rules. Humour doesn't travel well, so minimise it, concentrate on content and slow delivery, pocket the cheque and go home.*

17

Give yourself a hand

Without exception, the hands and arms are essential tools for the speaker.

They can help emphasise or de-emphasise
a point. They can be your best visual aids.

Even in a TV interview, where the subject is in close-up, you will be able to see the head, neck and upper shoulders of the speaker. Now, the next time you see one (tonight?), check out how many times another body part makes its presence felt on the screen – at least one hand and arm. Of course, for a waist-up, or full length vision of the speaker, you can see them anyway.

Your hands and arms can involve the audience, or push them back a bit. Not to use them is a capital offence for a speaker, so here's some advice.

First: what not to do. Most speakers are nervous at the start and ill-advised gestures can make this obvious to the audience. If you seek solace in gripping a lectern in front of you, it is surprising how many of the audience can see the whole thing shaking. Stroking a beard or a fringe, fidgeting with rings, scratching your nose – these all provide evidence of a nervous speaker. If you position yourself with your hands in your pockets, it might seem cool and relaxed to you, but it's crap position numero uno. For one thing, your hands are pressing in on your diaphragm,

Here's an idea for you...

It sounds vain but it's essential: use a mirror at home to establish your personal base position – and your strong gestures and/or visual-aid stuff. Work on your timing – gestures support your content, so make sure you do. This is also a good way to laugh at yourself, in case you start thinking you are a rock star.

restricting your breathing. You are also likely to interfere with any on-body microphone wiring. Finally, the only supporting gesture a man can make in these circumstances involves pocket billiards...

Here's what you should do with them. Forget your focus on the next speech – it is critically important that, as a speaker, you establish a base position for your hands and arms for all occasions that is comfortable for you, and provides a platform for the gestures you want to make, when you want to make them. This position will be personal to you, and reflect not only your speech content (for example, if you are holding notes or a visual-aid switch) but your style – whether you move or stand still, and whether you are laid-back or dramatic.

Here's what works for me. Try it and use it as a start to develop your own. As a speaker, I am not laid-back, and I move about. For the non-dramatic and stationary bits (linking and/or low emphasis stuff), I resort to my base position. I 'rest' both my elbows lightly on the side of my ribs, and point my lower arms out to the front, parallel to the ground. They lean toward each other, but do not touch. The fingers are loosely open. From that base position, I can hit any gesture – single or double-handed, right, left or forward, high or low. Try it, and develop it, or something like it, for yourself. Don't worry about feeling odd, or thinking you look odd – just remember, if you haven't established your own, you will look odder and feel worse.

Now, what do you do with your hands? I do not recommend that you hit the Italian end of the speaker/hand gesture spectrum; Italian speakers' hands never seem to stop. Whereas it works for the Italian language and culture, it probably won't for yours. But you should use your hands and arms emphatically for the following:

Go easy with the dramatic gestures when you're speaking overseas. A positive gesture in one place can be negative elsewhere. Look in IDEA 48, *Ich bin eine Berliner*, for ideas on cutting this risk.

Try another idea...

- When strong gestures are needed. Here's an example: I'm making a point that something in my speech refers to all employees in a company. I will pause, point forwards and upwards above my head, and indicate that there's the CEO. Slowly draw an invisible line downwards (finishing in a crouch) until you reach knee level. That's the janitor. Then, stand up, and from your base position widen your arms – to encompass the full breadth of the business. Do it slowly and nobody will miss the message.

- Use your hands for visual aids. Again, an example: if you have a graph with only five points of relevance on it, put your hand out in front of your face, fingers spread, and tell them that's a graph. Keep it up there, and tell them what the five-point scale is. You won't lose a person – but put the same stuff on a slide, and you'll lose half of them.

'Licence my roving hands and let them go...'
JOHN DONNE

Defining idea...

75

How did it go?

Q **I try everything to calm me down, but I am very nervous at the start of a speech. I'm desperate to hold on to something to stop shaking. Can you adapt or invent a base position to help?**

A *Yes – and, hey, it happens to all of us. Take my advised base position, and actually join your hands, loosely, so the backs of the hands face the audience. That's enough to stop them shaking. When you are ready, break them free.*

Q **I still get asked to use a hand-held microphone. Any advice on hand/arm gestures when you are doing that?**

A *To me, this is the worst option. If you hold other things (notes, etc.) at least you can move them about. A hand-held microphone needs to stay steady about 20 cm from your mouth. That's a real restriction for one hand – cutting your hand/arm gestures by half. Ask if the hand microphone will go on a stand, then go back to base.*

18

Moving target

The march of microphone technology has enabled speakers to add another potent weapon to their armoury: mobility.

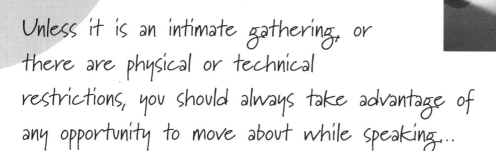

Unless it is an intimate gathering, or there are physical or technical restrictions, you should always take advantage of any opportunity to move about while speaking...

It widens the breadth of theatrical and dramatic actions available, and can energise your whole delivery.

This would have been entirely different if it had been written ten years ago... cast your mind back over recent show-business history. Remember Elvis, wiggling away but rooted to the same spot in front of a stand microphone? Then think about Tom Jones, a bit later, mobile but inhibited by having to hold a hand microphone. Now think about Madonna today, energetically dancing all over the stage, her singing picked up by a tiny radio microphone over her ear. There is simply no technical restriction caused by microphone and/or sound system factors. Such is the march of technology, and its attendant price reductions, that these systems are generally available at most event locations now. If you have a chance to do a Madonna, take it

Here's an idea for you...

I promise I'm not on a percentage and this idea will cost you a bit of cash, though not a lot. Buy any Robin Williams stand-up performance on DVD. Half of the verbal content may well go over your head, but just focus on his mobility. He is frenetic, and his energy level alone sucks you in to enjoy his performance. Now, imagine him doing that standing still.

– albeit without copying all the details of her stage act. Obviously, you don't have to move about, but the opportunity is there to add a new and rewarding dimension to your speech.

Moving about adds energy to your delivery. It is not always appropriate – for example, if you are addressing a very intimate meeting, neither you nor the audience will want the same energy level you would employ if you were on stage in front of 1,000 people. On the other hand, if you are speaking for anything over half an hour, your perceived energy as a speaker becomes critical in keeping the audience interested. It is a misconception that loudness alone gives impact.

Obviously, the combination of the room set-up and the available microphone/sound system will govern whether you are Elvis (c. 1968) or Eminem (c. 2005), but don't underestimate your ability to influence these factors – either in the run-up briefing discussions or on the day, when you arrive. Use these processes to give yourself the most flexibility, even if you don't plan to use it all.

Let's assume you give yourself room for movement. Here are some ideas on how to make your mobility work well for your speech.

Look at IDEA 8, *The feng-shui factor*, for thoughts on getting the best room set-up for you.

Try another idea…

- Even if you are provided with a full Madonna kit, you will have limitations on your movement. Find out beforehand what they are. If the organisers are videoing the session (increasingly popular) there will be limits on where you can move. The position of the speakers also needs noting – you need to work with the sound man to avoid going into areas which suddenly create screaming feedback. If you've got the chance, mark your limits on the stage floor with some masking tape.
- In the same way you have established a base position for your body posture, establish a base position on the stage area. This might be as simple as where your water glass is, or your notes (or whatever), but it is a place where you can pause, take stock, gather your thoughts, link one section to another and then set off again.
- Give nobody any peace! Use your ability to move to get real eye contact with as much of the audience as possible. Early on in your speech, move to your left-hand limit, and find a friendly, receptive face in the audience. Then deliver your speech as though you were talking to him or her for a minute or so. Then move to the centre, and ditto. Then to the right extreme, and ditto again. Repeat until you've finished.

'These boots were made for walking…'
LEE HAZELWOOD

Defining idea…

Q **I am booked to give an after-dinner speech, and have ascertained I will have a mobile 'clip-on' radio-microphone. I have also seen a room plan, and there are ten tables of ten. There seems nothing to stop me moving about between all the tables while speaking. Is this idea just too ambitious and risky?**

A *Not necessarily. It can be incredibly effective, but not all speakers are comfortable with such an unstructured approach. I would establish a stage area (any visible free space will do), and then use the front two or three tables as part of your stage. A master of the 'walkabout' is Tom Peters, the business guru. Amazingly, he's always near the exit when his speech finishes!*

Q **I have seen occasional speakers and performers who seem to succeed because they are deliberately miserable and stationary. They deliver their stories, messages and punchlines without a smile or any movement – but they seem to have a great impact. I am an introvert by nature, but enjoy speaking. Could this approach work for me?**

A *It might, but you would be choosing the hardest route for both you and your audiences. Sure, there are 'doleful' performers – but the (very few) successful ones tend to be stand-up comedians working in particular niches. It is a very specialist delivery style which needs very special material – and an audience that is probably expecting both.*

19

Hello Honkies

With some trepidation, let's venture into the subject of including slang and/or swear words in your speech...

Most reference books are crystal-clear in their advice: leave it out. I differ.

Used sparingly and sensibly in most speeches, a well-chosen swear word or piece of slang can have three times the effect of any sanitised equivalent.

Times have changed. Whether you treat it as good news or bad news, it is a fact that people both use and accept profanity and slang on a much more widespread basis than ever before. Unless you are facing an audience of 'born-agains' it is not only possible to use and get away with a sprinkling of Class B profanities – it is likely you will lose some potential impact if you do not.

The words 'sprinkling' and 'Class B' are the important ones in the last sentence. I'm talking about one, two or three in a forty-minute speech, and I am not talking about the 'serious' four letter words. With the 'progress' we are making, the time may come when these will be acceptable, but for now they have no place in any speech I can envisage you giving – even if it is a bit wild and after dinner. Mitch Murray, in his excellent *Handbook for the Terrified Speaker*, suggests that in most

Here's an idea for you…

Try alluding to very rude words without actually using them. A few years ago, I was working with Tom Peters. Prior to us both going onstage he mentioned that he'd just been in one of my company restaurants. Everything had been OK, but the whole experience was (I quote), 'Ho fucking hum'. It was a very powerful business point (i.e. when you do it right, it's still ordinary) and we decided to use it, and I have used it since. I will (with a smile) either call it 'HFH' – explaining what the first and last words are, but noting that 'the middle word begins with an "f" and I can't use that here in Cheltenham'. I have never openly used the word in question. I have never had to. It always works as a combination of a powerful point and a bit of fun, and it wouldn't do so without being rude.

settings you can safely use words like 'pissed', 'bullshit', 'crap' and 'bonk' – and I would agree, adding 'bollocks' as a personal favourite. And I'm now sitting at my keyboard wondering if anybody has ever previously written a single sentence which contained all those words.

This all comes down to you and your judgement. If you are not comfortable in normal life with a few rude expressions or slang words, then leave them out. If you don't mind a few of either or both, and judge the audience and occasion to be suitably receptive, go with a sprinkling. What is important is that this is used solely to support and enhance your content. Do not use it just for its shock effect – and there really is no place for common vulgarity, 'lavatorial' humour or sexual references in most speeches.

Here's an example of how it can work. My Manchester accent confuses most Americans, who believe all Brits speak like Prince Charles. I use an occasional anecdote to have a bit of fun with this. Without covering the whole story, I'm in a restaurant and have a problem. I explain it to the waiter, adding that I don't want my money back, I'm OK generally with what's happened; I just want to point this problem out. He insists on getting the manager. The manager arrives, and listens to the start of my story. He then – literally – jumps backwards and says, 'You're Australian'. Depending on my audience, I will then say 'That ticked me off, so I changed my mind and demanded my money back', or 'That really pissed me off and I demanded my money back'. I choose the version depending on my judgement as to whether the audience will understand the humour – that mistaking a Brit for an Aussie (and vice versa) is an insult, which they get everywhere but the US – but my point is that invariably the audience responses to the two versions are very different. The ruder one, if I've judged it right, brings the audience to life. The sanitised one gets a bit of a giggle.

For some ideas on handling risqué material with different sex audiences, look at IDEA 3, *Anyone here from outta town?*

Try another idea…

'Slang is a language that rolls up its sleeves, spits on its hands and goes to work.'
CARL SANDBURG, US author

Defining idea…

83

How did it go?

Q   **I am booked to speak at a sporting event, which will be a largely male audience with a lot of drink present. Do I simply go to the 'blue book' as the old music-hall comic Max Miller once called it – and tell filthy jokes?**

A   *Absolutely not. In the first place, you will not have been booked for that (though it's possible that somebody else has). In the 'range' of use of swear and slang words we have talked about above, push it towards your edge, but no further.*

Q   **I was told that a good way to figure out what you can and can't say is to write your speech and then pretend you have your mother in the audience. If she'd be embarrassed, by something, cut it out. Is this good advice?**

A   *The obvious answer is that it depends on your mum. Peter Kay, the UK stand-up, often has his mother in the audience and gets away with occasional blue murder (emphasis on the blue). My mother would hit me with her umbrella if I went that far. But I think it is a good idea to try and define who the most sensitive member of your upcoming audience might be, and then listen to your proposed speech again, as though it was through their ears. If you get dizzy through squirming, get back to the drawing board.*

20

Did everyone hear that?

Dealing with hecklers is something unlikely to apply to you unless you are considering a career in stand-up comedy. But just in case...

Heckling is not as frightening as it sounds.

For one thing, it happens very rarely outside the professional comedy club circuit. If it does, it is as much an opportunity for a speaker as it is a problem – based on the premise that hecklers are not usually very bright or sober.

I am indebted to the UK stand-up Frank Skinner for the chance for me – without shame – to quote from his autobiography his all-time favourite heckle. He was playing the Red Rose Club in North London, and about two minutes into his act a blind man shouted, 'Get off you Brummie bastard. [Pause] Has he gone yet?' I'll be honest with you – if you receive a heckle that funny and clever, then hold your hands up and surrender. Invite the guy on stage, give him the microphone and go and sit in his place. Everybody will be better off.

Here's an idea for you...

Plan to draw the fire of any audiences in advance by saying something like this: 'As we are really tight for time I would appreciate it if you could keep any questions or comments – including yells for me to go home or get 'em off – until afterwards, when I'll be at the coffee counter outside.'

Now let's take the subject seriously for a minute. Heckling – and other unhelpful, irritating audience interruptions – can happen, and it is as well to be prepared so you are not thrown from your horse and/or you do not 'lose' the goodwill of the audience. Either or both can easily happen.

Unless it's late in the evening and alcohol has been liberally available, the most likely source of IAIs (Irritating Audience Interruptions) is likely to be from inside a medium-to-big audience, where some peer-group chemistry and the absence of a boss figure is making a group of (usually) guys frisky. You might also experience the loner – somebody who is pissed-off with the proceedings in general and decides to make his or her point(s) known while you are on stage. Whatever the source, it is unlikely that you will be the direct target – the audiences for a professional speaker are generally more considerate.

If you get an IAI, some interesting relationship dynamics occur. The audience starts out on your side. They, too, are irritated – the likelihood being that they hear too much of the heckling prat at other times. If it carries on, however, they will begin to take a neutral position. They want to see how you handle it. It's from this stage on that the risk comes in – if you handle it badly, they will switch sides. It's not a mortal wound, but it means that you start the rest of your speech 'journey' in a boat with the wind in your face.

So, how do you handle it well? How do you avoid handling it badly?

- If somebody, or a group of somebodies, starts getting noisy, do not start to speak louder in the hope you will drown the noise. Here's a trick: do the opposite and start to speak softly. There's a chance that the audience, suddenly straining to hear, will shut the guilty one(s) up. Sorted.

- Don't overreact to the odd IAI. In fact, don't react at all to the first couple, particularly if they are early on in your speech. Audiences do take time to settle and there is sometimes a bit of banter if a couple of latecomers arrive, or somebody sees somebody they haven't seen for a while. It's just static interference – ignore it and carry on. It will probably fade out as you and the audience settle.

- If it continues and it crosses a line where you believe it can't be ignored, don't get angry and don't get artificially clever. Either or both of these responses from you will see the audience flip sides – from supporting you to supporting the heckler. By artificially clever I mean you flipping out some pre-learned 'put-down' line as listed in an ancient comedy club guide to heckler squashing (like 'Isn't it a shame when cousins marry?'). Stay calm, grin and be gentle ('Look, I don't mind a bit of audience noise, but there's a lady up here in the front row trying to get some sleep.').

The potential for heckling increases with the presence of alcohol. For some more thoughts on speaking with booze around, try IDEA 26: *Ish a pleasure (hic) to be here.*

Try another idea…

'There is something of a myth about heckling. In fourteen years I have heard about three or four funny heckles. Mostly it's drunks shouting… or just making incomprehensible noise.'
FRANK SKINNER, UK comedian

Defining idea…

How did it go?

Q **I'd just started a recent speech and I got hit with a belter. It was a joke, shouted out from the back of the audience, at my expense (or at least, at the expense of where I came from, after that had been announced). It was genuinely funny and the whole audience roared. So did I. What should I have done?**

A *You did exactly right. You can't plan for these. Join the fun, use the created energy to your advantage, and get on with it. As Frank Skinner says, sometimes even Homer just had to nod.*

Q **What happens if it gets out of control, when the level of noise and interruptions make it impossible to deliver your speech?**

A *If this happens to you, whatever your client is paying you, you are in the wrong place. Do not try and take them all on, or get in a slanging match. Stay calm – but wrap up as quickly as possible. Then sit down or walk off, and let them recriminate amongst themselves – which they will do.*

21

Don't leave it on the training ground

A speech is like an iceberg. It's supported by something, made of the same material, that is many times its actual size.

That something is called rehearsal.

People often come to me after speeches and tell me how 'lucky' I am – probably due to Irish genes – to be able to give an 'impromptu' speech to large audiences. I have *never* given an impromptu professional speech. When people call me 'lucky' I am reminded of the golfer Gary Player's comments on the subject: 'It's funny, the more I practise, the luckier I get'. Only my wife knows about the hours of rehearsal that go into an 'impromptu' speech of forty-five minutes without notes.

There is no substitute for rehearsal – but it should be time well spent. Too much of the wrong sort of rehearsal can work the other way. Here are a couple of things I've learned to avoid:

- Often in business-based events, you will be invited to 'rehearse' your speech. This is a largely because the boss will have allowed a 'window' in their busy schedule to run through their presentation in front of the PR manager

Here's an idea for you...

An audio recorder is a useful aid. Get your speech sections onto a CD or tape – it does help to get the timing right for each section. A few replays will help you to remember the contents triggered by your key words or phrases.

and some wannabes. It will be hinted that you 'might like' to attend in order to 'run through' your 'presentation'. Refuse politely. You should certainly get access to the stage to check out your microphone and range of movements, but do not attempt to give your speech to an auditorium that is empty apart from this lot. You cannot recreate the real thing in a rehearsal, and you will just knock your confidence – and theirs – by trying.

■ Do not try and learn large chunks of your speech verbatim. If you need to be exact (e.g. if you are quoting somebody) then make no bones about it during the speech – read it from a piece of paper. If you do attempt to remember too much, the memorising takes all your energy and you become a Johnny-one-note.

Rehearse your speech in real time. It is not about doing it in front of a mirror – that's useful for practising gestures and posture. This is about rehearsing for a specific speech and event. You need an imaginary audience, and it is not about any

one aspect of your style and/or content, but the totality. Is the balance right within the whole? Are you meeting your success criteria for the speech? Is there enough impact to make the key points memorable? Is the timing right

To help you rely on your memory more, and your notes less, look at IDEA 24, *Marvo the Memory Man.*

Try another idea...

when you do it in real time? (Always plan for your speech to last a little less time than you are allowed – however 'real' your rehearsals are, you always tend to underestimate audience response and reaction time.)

Even if you do not plan to use notes, start your rehearsals by writing down as many key words and/or phrases as you need to cover all bases. Then whittle the notes down to your comfortable minimum key words or phrases. When you've got to this stage, rehearse each section as and when you can. Without moving into parrot mode, rehearse it from a key word trigger so that you know how long it takes on average. If you do it this way, you can use up a lot of short bits of spare time – in the car, in the gym, having a jog, etc.

Repeat the above until you are sure of yourself. There are no short cuts…

'*Amateurs practise until they can get it right. Professionals practice until they can't get it wrong.*'
HAROLD CRAXTON, Professor at the Royal Academy of Music

Defining idea...

How did it go?

Q I am a bit cautious and nervous by nature, but quite good on my feet when I get going. I tend to rehearse and rehearse – and then find I'm going through the motions when I stand up on the day. Is it possible to overdo it?

A *At first sight, what I am about to say seems to go against everything that's been written above – but I don't think it is. It is possible to over-rehearse. It is a common problem, and it can inhibit good delivery. With each individual this is going to be different, and it will only become clear after some time and experience on your feet – but you need to stop rehearsing when you are comfortable and confident. You must retain the ability to make it sound fresh, and give yourself some flexibility in style and content on the day. Otherwise you won't enjoy it, and it will show.*

Q Before I go on I tend to keep (silently) repeating my full content of key words and phrases. If I'm sure of them, I'm more confident when I start. Is that the best way to use any 'dead' time just before you go on?

A *Each to his or her own here. The time right before your speech is often 'dead' to you – there may be somebody else speaking, or the audience is assembling: whatever. It's a time for you to try and relax and strengthen your own confidence, and one way of doing this is to reassure yourself that you can regurgitate your trigger words. I have a different routine: I concentrate on my opening. However calm and/or cocky you are, the first couple of minutes on stage are all about appearing calm while nervous – and I just make sure my opening (which usually differs for each speech) is at the top of my mind as I go on.*

22

It's a wrap

The audience is ready. Your mind is full of trigger words and phrases. Right there, right then, the organiser comes up to you and asks you to cut fifteen minutes...

Adaptability is key.

The combination of an audience, venue, sound system – plus a gaggle of 'lesser' variables like catering – in one place at one time add up to a lot of things that can go wrong. A good speaker can become part of the solution.

It is almost always an adjustment of time that is required – and that's usually about shortening your speech as things are 'running late'. If you see this happening, for goodness sake, intervene and volunteer. You will score points with all parties. At the scheduled start time of a recent speech in Johannesburg, we were still a couple of hundred delegates missing due to traffic problems. I suggested to the beleaguered organiser that I'd slice fifteen minutes off as a contribution to the pool of things that were being considered to get the day back on track. I almost got a kiss on the lips, which was disconcerting as the organiser was a 250 lb male Afrikaner.

Here's an idea for you...

The other speaker hasn't turned up – and the organisers have thirty blank minutes to fill. You can pre-plan for such an emergency contingency, and help out to a point. Use your alternate segment theory to bring in a couple of finite segments from your mental 'substitutes bench' – but be warned. I would never take on more than ten or fifteen minutes additional responsibility like this. Beyond that, everybody suffers and you solve nothing.

This is something you can rehearse. I have a strange role model for this – Phil Mickelson, the American golfer. When he shows up for one of the majors, and goes about his practice rounds, he often doesn't bother driving off the tee. In his mind a tee shot is a tee shot and you can practise those on the range. What he does is walk up the fairway, and practise approaching the pin from a range of distances and angles. In short, he practises finishing from different positions.

A very useful activity for you is to practise moving to your finish from different stages of your speech. There are core elements common to all my speeches and, once I have put a 'backbone' together for a specific speech, I identify at least three ways of 'approaching the green'. If you are called on to make a deep cut, this does not just mean working back through your sequenced trigger points in reverse order (i.e. drop the one before the ending, then drop the one before that, etc.). It may be that you need to omit something near the start.

I call this my alternate segment theory. If you did maths at school, you may remember this as a confusing idea that implied some relationship between the angles created by lines drawn across circles. You will never have had any practical use for such pish – but, as a speaker, you will find my AS theory invaluable. When you build and rehearse a speech, you know that sections of it are triggered by key words or phrases. It is these sections (segments) that give you the flexibility to adapt to any demands to change your timing (or content). Don't try and speed up the whole, and don't try and take out bits of this and bits of that. Design your segments so that you can leave them out (or put them in) in holistic fashion. If you have ten such segments in your speech, and you are faced with a deep cut, in your mind that model will already be designed as missing out numbers three and seven, and going straight from six to finish with eight, nine and ten.

For more help in structuring 'segments' so they can be used holistically and flexibly, see IDEA 14, *One step at a time*.

Try another idea...

'If it be now, 'tis not to come; If it is not to come, it will be now; If it be not now, yet will it come: The readiness is all.'
WILLIAM SHAKESPEARE, *Hamlet*

Defining idea...

How did it go?

Q **I gave a speech recently, and everything was on schedule. My timing was spot on, but suddenly I started getting 'cut' signals from the organiser. I ignored them to start with, but got flustered as the signs continued – so I suddenly wound up and sat down. I feel I came out of it looking bad. Is there anything I could have done to handle it better?**

A *Clearly, if everything was on track when you started your speech, and you were on track during it, something untoward happened. In that case, I would just stop the show and seek clarification – explaining to the audience that you are getting signs that something has happened. Let any redirection come from the mouths of the organisers. Use the pause to settle yourself and then do what you can to respond to the changed circumstances. The audience will be on your side.*

Q **I followed the speaker from hell. He was supposed to have a ten-minute slot, and then introduce me. He stayed on his feet for twenty-five minutes. Should I have made cuts to try and make the time up? Or should I have run with what I was booked for?**

A *Assuming you got no redirection from the organisers, then if it's early in the day I would give the speech you planned to give. If it's the last session, I would not overrun without reference to the organisers. However, if you are delayed significantly by a previous speaker, and nobody offers guidance, then I would consider it fair and sensible to get open clarification (over the microphone if necessary) about the changed timing. In that way, the audience knows an overrun is down to somebody else's inadequacy and not your ego.*

23

I'm sorry, I'll read that again

Handled well, using notes can strengthen your confidence, ensure the presence and sequence of your speech's key points and enhance the impact of its delivery.

Handled badly, using notes can inhibit all three...

I never refer to notes during a speech. But I always have them, specifically written for that speech, in my inside pocket. So should you, and you should have no qualms about using them. There is no shame in using notes. Most speakers do – and should – use them. But they should not dominate you, or your performance. They should support both.

I carry notes for two reasons. The first is that I've done the work, so why wouldn't I? I condense my key trigger words and phrases onto the back of a standard-sized envelope. The second reason is that I am fifty-eight, with a remarkable aptitude to remember the line-up of 1960s Manchester-based pop groups, but a remarkable inability to remember somebody I met last week. My notes are in my pocket just in case my memory fails me.

Is there any occasion where it is justified to read a full presentation to an audience? Short answer: no. The vast majority of public-speaking occasions are not about the

Here's an idea for you...

If you do have to read something out, clearly mark where you pause – even for how long – and the words you want to emphasise (for example, with colours or by underlining). This will enable you to offset the natural loss of oratory variation you tend to get when reading out loud.

exactitude of the words. If you were to read a full presentation to an audience, most of them would actually be insulted, and when you finally looked up at the end you would probably find them gone. If your eyes are away from the audience you lose 80% of the potential magic.

It is not uncommon, however, to have to read out bits verbatim. If there is a part that you feel might get a wider audience after the speech, you may want to make sure you are quoted correctly. If your speech has some academic content, you will want to be sure you get the details right. You may want to refer to a printed article that supports your speech, in which case it is better to have the specific text to hand. In all these cases you will need to read out bits, and that's not a problem. It can be quite theatrical if you do it properly – but do not rely on the original document; there's a good chance you will not be able to read it in half light. Type it, or print it out again, in capital letters, double-spaced and (at least) an 18 point font. If you don't know what that looks like:

IT LOOKS LIKE THIS.

If it carries onto more than one page, end each page at a sentence or paragraph end – and, preferably, where a pause will work. Number your pages because, yes, one day you will drop them.

Notes in the form of cue cards get the job done. I end up with one 'card' – my envelope – but I would recommend that you use the model I see most on the speaking circuit, a series of smaller cards (about postcard size) held in one hand. In this way, your movements and microphone use are not inhibited at all.

If you do need to read something, look up IDEA 33 on using Autocue: *I seem to have moved from 33 to 45 rpm.*

Try another idea...

Use as many cards as you have segments. I'm stressing 'card' – not paper. Condense each segment into a trigger word for a heading at the top of each card, and then add no more than a handful of bullet points. Do not try and put too much content on a card – that deadly silence when you look back to your notes and try and find where you left off is a killer if you've just built up momentum. Write only on one side of the card. Punch a hole in the same place in the top left hand corner of each, and link them by what are sometimes called Treasury tags (two metal pins connected by a bit of string). In that way, if you drop them, they remain in order. When, during the speech, you move from one segment to another, slide the used card from the front to the back. Practise this a few times – it's not as straightforward as it seems.

'The notes I handle no better than many pianists. But ... between the notes – ah, that is where the art resides.'
ARTUR SCHNEBEL

Defining idea...

How did
it go?

Q **I read about the controversy when President Bush supposedly had a sort of radio-hearing-aid (with the battery pack visible under the back of his jacket). In this age of chip technology, are there electronic aids that could feed you your key words and reminders in some way without the audience knowing?**

A *There must be, but in my judgement they are not for the likes of you and me. I am reminded of Charlie Chaplin's sketch where he writes down song lyrics on his shirt cuff. During the song, as he gives a dramatic gesture, the cuff flies off across the room. If it's high-tech, it can go wrong – and that will leave you worse off. Remember KISS: Keep It Simple, Stupid.*

Q **I write my speeches out in full beforehand, but when I read them, it doesn't sound like me. Although I like the confidence I get from learning big chunks of it, am I losing something by this method?**

A *There is a big (and increasing) gap between written and spoken English – for example, when did you last say 'whom'? That's why I don't like writing a speech out in full, and/or learning parts of it parrot-fashion. Relax, and rely on your own everyday articulation and use of the language to deliver your speech.*

24

Marvo the Memory Man

To stand in front of an audience and speak confidently without notes is impressive.

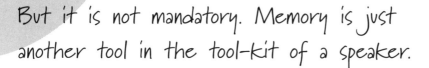

But it is not mandatory. Memory is just another tool in the tool-kit of a speaker.

If it's well used, the end product is the better for it. If it's badly used, the job can still get done properly – but will probably need assistance from something else. There is no better way of communicating and interacting with an audience than by never taking your eyes off those listening to (and watching) you. For a speaker to do this, it would seem to require an astonishing power of recall – and the confidence to rely on it.

I do not accept this. I *do* accept that some people seem to have a 'better' memory than others – but I do not accept that the level of memory needed to deliver a forty-minute speech qualifies the speaker to join a freak show. If you are contemplating taking public speaking seriously, then I assume that you have a reasonable level of self-confidence, articulation, presence and a fairly well-ordered mind. In which case, you have at least an average power of recall. You will certainly have enough to work up to a level where you can use it to help your performance. The mindset of a good speaker is not that lack of memory is a negative, but that the memory you do have is a positive.

Here's an idea for you...

This effectiveness of any memory-aiding technique can be enhanced by using colours. Try it on your speech material. If you consistently use a set of colours for sequencing your key points and phrases, it helps you to recall them in that order.

First of all, let me re-emphasise that I'm not talking about learning a speech parrot-fashion. There isn't a more counter-productive practice available to a speaker. We are talking about simple techniques that can be learned, and can help you recall key trigger words and phrases in your speech – and then some 'directional pointers' under each one to set you off on the 'subcontent'.

I invented the way I do this when I was sixteen at school. It was an early version of Windows. I would reduce a history essay to about six or seven key words (subheadings) and memorise them. Then I would pull up one of the key words in my memory, and – like Windows – drop down a submenu of a few bullet points for each one. When I reached each point in the submenu in the exam, I'd usually remember some vivid action or weird fact and expand on that. In a nutshell, that's how I remember a speech.

Try another idea...

Whatever techniques you use to help your memory, they are all helped if you feel confident. For more ideas on this try IDEA 28, *You're so vain*.

I've added to my basic 'windows' memory techniques, with some very sophisticated upgrades. The basic segments of my speech are the windows and submenus, but to make sure I get the sequencing right, I have added the Hopscotch Factor. It's a visual way of helping you recall the order you pull down your windows. If you remember your school playground, part was always covered in chalk marks – outlining little hopscotch 'courts'. There were usually about ten numbered squares, going out in groups of one, two or three. It would look something like this:

```
          1
      2       3
          4
  5       6       7
          8
      9       10
```

I put my key words and phrases into that sort of visual sequence diagram in my mind. Ten of these segments should cover most sequences. If a linear ten is too many, add (yet) another of my 'upgrades' – the 'Max Hastings' technique. He was the journalist who famously commented on the safe return of British fighter planes during the Falklands War: 'I counted them all out, and I counted them all back in.' In this version, you set off on the visual hopscotch, but count only five points out, and then five back again. This version would be pictured in your mind like this:

Start: 1 2 3 4 5 … 5 4 3 2 1 :Finish

Try one, or a combination of these a few times with the content of your next speech – you will be amazed at your power of recall. You may find yourself confident enough to do the speech with just one summary cue card, or – like me – with one cue card in your inside pocket for system-failure situations.

'Memories are not shackles,
they are garlands.'
ALAN BENNETT

Defining
idea…

How did it go?

Q **I have just had a horrible experience – a complete memory system shut-down half way through a speech. By the time I got back on track, I felt I had lost the audience. How can you manage this kind of crisis?**

A *The first thing to remember is that it will not be as big a deal to the audience as it is to you – so don't panic. Something like that happened to me once in front of 15,000 people in L.A., but when I saw a video afterwards, nothing untoward seemed to have happened. Follow the advice given for computer operating systems when they freeze – just switch off and start again. Take a drink of water, and go back to the first key trigger point in your mind and start the sequence again in summary, in your mind. It may take you twenty seconds to get back into the flow – but you will.*

Q **I'm OK with memorising content, but hopeless at tracking time. A speaker I know gets a friendly member of the audience to give him signals as time passes. Would this help me?**

A *I doubt it. If you are looking the other way and miss one, the whole thing could go wrong. You should try and stay in control of all the key variables, including time management. Always wear a watch, and if you keep forgetting to look at it, take it off and leave it by your water glass.*

25

Can you tell what it is yet?

**I don't like visual aids, but I confess that occasionally –
and I stress that last word – I quite like speaking
accompanied by a flip chart. It's the Rolf Harris in me...**

In intimate surroundings — say an audience
of less than twenty-five — the creative use of
a flip chart can add to the entertainment,
impact and memorability of a speech and speaker.

Where, I suspect, I differ from most speakers on this subject is that, if I had to choose one of those three values that I suggest can be added by working with a flip chart, it would be entertainment. I don't fall into the camp of filling a flip chart with tiny writing while the enthralled audience stares at my bum.

I've already suggested this only works in intimate venues, and I'd still use it sparingly. If I felt I could complement something I wanted to say, rather than conflict with it, I'd give it a go. If I had a complex bit of content, for example, and wanted to summarise it in one or two key points so that the audience would remember those, I'd use one. If I had a short powerful idea, I'd use it. As an example of this kind of content, I have pinched Einstein's $E=MC^2$ formula a couple of times. He used it to help explain some of the world's previously unanswered questions,

Here's an idea for you...

Choose your venue and audience carefully for this kind of thing, but I have seen a speaker substitute a big bed-sheet for a flip chart, and an aerosol spray-paint can for a felt-tip pen. It obviously needs pre-staging as the sheet has to be vertically stretched and fixed, but every now and again the speaker would pause and spray a summary word, phrase or symbol on to the sheet in magnificent graffiti-style lettering. At the end he had the best visual aid I've ever seen. No, I've never tried it, and I suggest you would need to rehearse this kind of thing a lot. If you do, do not send me your laundry bill.

whereas in my case I use it to make the point that (business) Efficiency (E) comes when you combine Motivation (M) and Commitment (C). If I do my Rolf Harris bit with those three simple letters, it makes it much more memorable.

If you do use a flip chart, here are ten ideas which are worth remembering:

- Bring one with you. Do not rely on the hosts.
- If you write live (as against having it pre-written), try and keep half-facing the audience while you do it. In that way your speech is still all about you, and your visual aid is not conflicting.
- Check the room out beforehand – can people read your printing from the furthest vantage point?
- You can print out your flip charts beforehand. This enables you to spend a bit of time on it. In which case, leave the top sheet blank. During the speech, when you've finished with a sheet, turn it over or rip it off, and make sure the next one is blank, with your next printed sheet below that – and so on. If you want to tear it off, pre-score it at the top.
- Writing it out beforehand avoids the dreaded **COMMUNIC**ATION syndrome – where you start out with a big confident letter and then realise you haven't enough space to complete the word...

- If you rely on the felt-tip pens provided by the venue, they will almost certainly be too thin (or knackered). Buy one with at least a 2.5 cm (1 in) 'nib' beforehand. Actually, buy three – it adds impact if you use different colours on a chart.
- Always write words horizontally, even if you are showing a summary graph with a vertical axis.
- If you have a few pages of flip charts, mark each one 'index style' with a sticky note that you can read (in case you have to go straight to a particular one or cut one out).
- Leave each page up for at least a minute (even if it is only $E=MC^2$).
- If you want the 'theatrical' impact of writing (or even drawing) something on a flip-chart in front of an audience, do it lightly in pencil beforehand.

For more ideas on working with slides (and the dangers therein), try IDEA 30, *You can look at me or look at that.*

Try another idea…

'It's amazing what you can do with an E in A-level art, a twisted imagination and a chainsaw.'
DAMIEN HIRST

Defining idea…

How did it go?

Q **For bigger audiences can you get the same effectiveness as a flip chart by writing – in real time – on overhead transparencies?**

A *Not in my book. It takes away the focus from you to a 'competing' screen. It means you have to stop and (partly) darken the room. It means you have to focus on writing on an A4-sized sheet, with a clumsy pen while the audience watches your nib movements, your shaky fingers and your spelling. If it's a big audience and you need a visual aid, use pre-prepared slides and a proper AV system.*

Q **I use a flip chart for certain summary points, and put a few helpful descriptive notes in light pencil at my eye level on the chart. Is this a bit of a giveaway with an intimate audience?**

A *If it is, it doesn't matter. What matters is the overall content of the speech and style of the speaker – and you get both right by being confident. If this helps your confidence, score ten out of ten for originality.*

26

Ish a pleasure (hic) to be here

The issues of managing and responding to the excesses of alcohol are important for a speaker – and are getting more so.

I enjoy my pint(s), and have been known, on occasion, to get myself outside rather too much claret... but never before a speaking engagement.

With an audience, a reasonable amount of alcohol can make them more relaxed, and receptive – which can help a speaker. An unreasonable amount can work the other way. For a speaker, no amount of alcohol can make you more effective or efficient.

Why should this be an issue? Surely the role of the speaker is to turn up to an event, act professionally, do the job and ride off into the sunset. If there is booze around, that's somebody else's prerogative. Just don't get pissed and, if the audience does get a bit frisky, whack a couple of rude jokes in and Bob's your uncle.

It's not that simple. In twelve years of giving professional speeches, largely to business audiences, I have noticed that the presence and effect of alcohol is

Here's an idea for you...

Don't feel under pressure to 'join in the fun' when alcohol is present. That's nonsense. The audience knows what you are there for, and will respect your professionalism. What can work well is to have a bit of (self-deprecating) fun with your (seemingly) abstemious lifestyle. Try this: early on in the speech, pause for five seconds, s-l-o-w-l-y pour yourself a glass of water, smile faintly and say: 'I'm drinking tonic water right now – so that after the speech I can just drink neat gin.' It works wonders.

becoming more widespread. It may be that, because I use humour a lot, I get pushed towards the cocktail hour and after dinner. For whatever reason, however, I find myself thinking more about 'managing' the way alcohol is served at an event where I am speaking. There are two issues involved: a) avoiding it myself and b) trying to keep the audience intake at the right level and at the right time. If either or both of those go wrong, unreliable forces take over.

Let's deal with the issue of self-control first – and start by asking the question of why it is necessary. Every speaker suffers from 'pre-match' nerves, and surely an innocent gin and tonic before you go on will help settle those nerves and work to your advantage? Not in my book it won't, and you can take it from me that I am as tempted as any. Prior to a speech, you are high with adrenalin – and drinking has the same kind of effect on you that it has when you imbibe at an altitude of 35,000 feet in a plane. You will also need your best available clarity of thought and power of recall during your speech, and the innocent drink helps neither. What it *does* help is the propensity to have another.

If you are a guest speaker, if the event is purely social, or at the social end of the day, you will be invited to join the cocktails and/or drinks with dinner. My advice is to abstain, but drink plenty of water to avoid the dry mouth associated with nerves. In all my experience, I have only seen one speaker handle alcohol well. That was

Alex Hay, the ex-golfer and now TV pundit. If he reads this, it is meant as a compliment. Many years ago I shared a top table with him and he cheerfully downed a good chunk of the previous year's Burgundy output before giving a

If you do have trouble with a bit of drink-induced heckling, try IDEA 20: *Did everyone hear that?*

Try another idea...

quite magnificent after-dinner speech. I don't know whether it was a habit, or a one-off result of my over-dinner chat, but I quote him only as an exception that proves the rule. Everybody else I have seen try it has suffered, and some cringingly so.

If alcohol is present at the event, you can have some effect in getting the amount and timing organised in a way that might help your speech. Talk to the organiser and – if possible – whoever is in charge of the food and drink service. Try and get agreement to the following:

- Don't have drinks being served while you are speaking. Apart from the deflection for both you and the audience of people getting up and down and/or waiters moving about, it will also least ensure that the drinking momentum slows.

- If you are speaking after dinner, make sure that the MC makes an announcement, about ten minutes before you are introduced, to the effect that you are on the radar screen and this would be a good time for a 'comfort break'. Again, this alters the audience mindset and slows the drinking momentum down.

- If wine has been available with dinner, and liqueurs and brandies are due up, see if you can slot in after the first but before the second.

'Sherry gives rise to no thoughts.'
R. DRUITT, quoted in Geoffrey Madan's *Notebooks*

Defining idea...

113

How did it go?

Q **I'm slated to give a best-man's speech at a wedding. Surely you can't be expected to avoid all the drinking – what with the toasts and all that?**

A *My answer is guided by what you want folks to remember about you, your speech and the day. If you want to be remembered as a witty, bright, articulate and (acceptably) risqué speaker, follow my advice. If you want to be remembered as a crude, cringingly embarrassing, hugely unfunny idiot, get rat-arsed beforehand. Your choice.*

Q **Presumably it's OK to join in the fun after your speech?**

A *Absolutely! There are a few jobs left for you to do (perhaps explore repeat business possibilities) but you can now cross the great speaker–audience divide. I have been known, during my pre-speech 'organising' chats with the catering managers, to slip them some money to ensure a half bottle would still be available when I got back to my table.*

27

Hands up those who...

**Used carefully, the tactic of suddenly involving an
audience can help to cement their relationship with you.**

A speaker provides a multi-dimensioned
offering to an audience — encompassing
sight, sound and movement.

There is one more dimension that is available that can also impact on an audience –
its own involvement. This can serve as a device to ensure that one or more key
points really do stick in the memory.

The first point to make about using this tactic is that its effectiveness is correlated
to the size and intimacy of the audience and/or room. It works best in small spaces,
where the members of the audience can hear each other. It works even better in
such a venue if you, the speaker, can move about and address one or more
members of the audience on a one-to-one basis.

Involving the audience really boils down to asking a carefully posed question. The
purpose of using this tactic to support the impact of your speech is not to get the
answer per se, but to use the answer, and to use the two-way process, as devices to
create impact (to emphasise a key point) and entertainment (to change the speed,
attitude, climate and dimension of the room and event).

Here's an idea for you...

If you are unhappy at the thought of any one-on-one interactivity, or the audience is just too big for it, you can get much of the same effect by going for a show of hands against some (carefully designed!) multiple-choice questions. For example, if the question is, 'How long would it take for one person to count a billion one euro coins?', you might start by asking those of the audience who thought it might take 'between eight and twelve weeks' to count a billion coins to raise their hands. You'll get some, I promise. Then, offer a couple more categories. Then hit them with the answer. You'll miss the banter and the individuals, but you'll get the impact.

Here's an example. Sometimes, in a business speech, I want to make the point that bad leadership can be expensive to a business. I could use the example of the merger between Time Warner and AOL, which cost – literally – hundreds of billions of dollars in lost shareholder value. The problem with just reeling that off as a fact is that people have become anaesthetised to the idea of a billion (which, just to refresh your memory, is a thousand million). In business and public life, billions are bandied about as loose change. So, to get impact – and provide a bit of entertainment – in the right audience set-up, I will wander towards the front row, and ask the simple question: 'How long would it take for one person to count a billion one-pound coins or one-dollar notes?' You'll get a bit of fun ('How many times can you go to the toilet?' etc.,) and a range of answers. Some clever dick will realise it's going to be a surprising figure, so will shoot high – 'Maybe, er… eighteen months!' (Giggle, giggle.)

Then you give the answer – sixteen years.

Three things have happened here:

If you want to involve the
audience by having them ask
you questions, look up IDEA 45:
You at the back. Yes, you...

*Try
another
idea...*

- The audience has had some fun. The clever
  folk will have tried to impress, the
  comedians will have chucked in the one-
  liners and a bit of banter will have ensued. The atmosphere is a bit lighter and
  the speaker has become less distant (literally and metaphorically).
- They have a piece of information they will remember – principally because they
  will want to repeat the sixteen-year thing in the pub that evening and look
  clever.
- When you, the speaker, bring back the speech to the point that bad leadership
  can be hugely expensive for a business, the idea begins to have real meaning and
  power. They'll remember the point you were making, if only by association.

Done in a controlled way, this is a very powerful tactic. It does not involve the
audience asking you questions, which requires you to think on your feet. It does not
involve you getting into two-way, unscripted, unstructured (and, therefore, risky)
conversations with a member (or members) of the audience. It is a process which
can be pre-planned, scripted and controlled by you. You don't have to be at the
charismatic, free-wheelin' end of the speaker-characteristic spectrum to do this – in
fact it's a very helpful and powerful tactic if you are at the other end.

'*The mere asking of a
question causes it to
disappear or to merge into
something else.*'
E. M. FORSTER

*Defining
idea...*

How did it go?

Q **I gave a presentation in a high-tech lecture theatre recently, and noticed that each seat had a remote, hand-held, interactive feedback facility. If the lecturer asked a multiple-choice question, the audience members pressed the button they felt was appropriate, and the collective answers were displayed on a graph, instantly, on a screen on stage. It seemed a bit clumsy when it was all explained to me, but could this be an effective tool for a speaker?**

A *I will sound like a Luddite here, but I would steer clear of these. I have seen them used half a dozen times, and each time I have felt the presentation was being structured around the technological support, and not the other way around. The 'show of hands' is ideal – it's fast, personal and non-deflective. And, remember, it's not the answer that's important – it's what you do with it.*

Q **Is the staged question from a 'friendly' audience member a helpful technique to get people involved and keep you in control?**

A *If we are talking during the speech, I see no benefits in this, as against you asking the question and controlling the process. If we are talking about afterwards, and there is a formal Q and A session, and it opens with a deadly silence – then as a starter it can be helpful.*

28

You're so vain

Public speaking is a performing art. The speaker is a performing artist. The combination works best if some of the real world is left at the stage door.

For the speaker, that can include an anti-gravitational level of self-confidence.

A speaker without self confidence is like a roast chicken: it tastes OK and it fills a need. A speaker with confidence is like *coq au vin:* it tastes wonderful and it is more than the sum of the parts.

You can fancy-up what's needed here. You can call it self-confidence, self-belief, sure-footedness or self-empowerment. I prefer to accept it for what it is – a short (and maybe artificial) injection of vanity.

I qualified these words with the idea that the need is a 'short (and maybe artificial) injection'. Public speaking is not a no-go area for the reserved and introvert, but it does require the ability to nip into a phone box on the way to the venue, put your underpants over your trousers and emerge as (in the words of Monty Python) 'something completely different' for the next couple of hours. The good news is that you can treat this like greasepaint – put it on and wipe it off after the performance.

Here's an idea for you…

You do need to feel cocky. It is important, however, that you do not let this manifest itself in disrespect for either the organising folk or the audience. Using your sure-footedness to give them confidence in, and respect for, you is one thing. They will be your friends. Using it to make them feel small is another. They will become enemies.

What is it that terrifies people about public speaking? It is, essentially, a two-part fear:

- The fear of the unknown. The obvious ones are the venue, the facilities, the audience, the reception, the response – but sometimes you can add to these things like travel logistics which can add to the overall stress level.
- The fear of making a fool of yourself. Maybe you are a rookie. Or maybe your style will be wrong for the audience. Your content might be misjudged. You will not know enough about your subject. Perhaps you will lose your notes and/or forget something and/or (aaarrrrggghhh!) dry up completely. Could the microphone fail? Ad infinitum…

There is nothing – nothing – in that lot that cannot be managed, overcome and controlled. You can take a few ideas from me, but your most powerful weapon is your own objectivity mixed with a few dos and don'ts:

- The hardest fears to overcome are those associated with inexperience. You are just not sure how to handle yourself and you are afraid it will show. But just pause before you drown under this wave. Picture, in your mind, your role-model performer. Now wind the picture back. That person was a rookie once – just imagine that. Then remember that they got through it, just as you will. There is a big difference between making mistakes and failing – just plan on making a few of the former. It's part of the journey.

The opening couple of minutes on stage are all about confidence. For some more ideas on openings, try IDEA 13: *Another opening, another show.*

Try another idea...

- When you get to the event, remember that your underpants are outside your trousers. You are SuperSpeaker. Take your opening conversations to the sound man, the organiser, the catering manager... Make it clear that you are sure-footed and you know what you want. They will look at you differently, and this feeds your self-confidence.

- If you are coming out from behind a curtain, make sure you get a feel for the room beforehand – and get a sight of it while the audience is getting ready. Every room full of people is unique. If you are familiar with it before you open, you remove one huge unknown that clutters your mind with fear.

- When you first see the audience, think about judo. The difference between judo and wrestling is that in the latter you pitch your own power against your opponents. In judo, you use your opponents' power back on them. Almost every member of the audience will respect the fact it is you and not them up on stage. Quietly, they are willing you to succeed. There is, therefore, an enormous positive force present in the room when you go on – so use their power to boost your confidence (and performance).

'If you haven't got an ego today, forget it.'
GIANNI VERSACE

Defining idea...

123

How did it go?

Q **I take a mild sedative medication, and was wondering if I should take an extra one half an hour before speaking to calm the nerves and help my confidence?**

A *If you are on prescribed medication I would do exactly what it says on the tin – no more, no less. If you are not on prescribed medication, I would strongly advise against popping an upper or a downer in before speaking. Anything that threatens your powers of recall or articulation should be avoided – and there are other ways to beat the nerves/confidence thing.*

Q **Is being confident enough to laugh at your own jokes a no-no?**

A *It can be quite the opposite. A lot of clever funny-story tellers end up laughing along with the audience, and if it's done right it is infectious. What you shouldn't do is announce that something is about to be funny ('I heard a funny story the other day...'). But it does help if you make it clear that you have switched from a serious bit and that this story still makes you smile.*

29

Here's an example I found in my hotel room

The march of technology has had a tremendous impact on visual aids. But let's spend a bit of time in the visual-aid equivalent of the Stone Age...

Small, low-technology 'props', produced from nowhere and used as supporting examples, can punch way above their weight in making a point memorable for an audience.

Remember the O.J. Simpson trial? Whatever you views about the outcome (and I agree with you), the most memorable point in the elongated process was when the defence produced a battered glove – a replica of the one supposedly worn by the murderer. In a silent court, O.J. tried to put it on. It wouldn't fit. In my mind that's the moment he got off.

In this complex digital age, there is something about the 'simple' and 'non-technical' that still impacts on people. The *Blair Witch* movie relied on the fact that it was 'home-made' for its power.

Here's an idea for you...

You don't have to rely on hotels and you don't have to be spontaneous. Start looking now for your own small, low-tech examples. Plan them into your speech and bring them with you. I have fun with a Swiss army watch, a golf ball personalised with my name on it – and you wouldn't believe the mischief I can get up to with a bar of (I'm not making this up) 'french-milled' soap I pinched from a Marriott in Chicago.

In our speaking world, I witnessed an example from one of the masters, Tom Peters. He was making a point that big brands sometimes get so 'big'-minded that they forget some of the basic stuff that the individual customer actually needs. It was an interesting point, but most of us were waiting for him to move on to the next one. Suddenly, from his pocket, he produced a tiny shampoo bottle from his hotel room. Of course, we could barely make out what it was, let alone read the brand name and writing on the tiny label. It didn't matter, he held it up anyway. He asked (rhetorically): who was the average user of this bottle? Answer: probably a middle-aged travelling businessman, who wore reading glasses. He asked (rhetorically): when was it likely to be used? Answer: by that guy, without his glasses, inside the shower stall, with the water running and everything steamed up. Verdict: when it was most likely to be used, by its most probable customer, it was impossible to read the label and distinguish it from the other two similarly sized bottles provided.

It was a long time ago when I witnessed this – but to this day I can remember the point he made: a big brand (it was Neutrogena), with all its product qualities and 'market distinction', had lost the plot when it came to basic customer needs. And why do I remember that? Because he produced, with no prior warning, a tiny plastic bottle that I could barely see.

This is not only a powerful idea, it's one you can have fun with. It's amazing what you can find in a hotel room if you are bored shitless on the night before a speech – and there are only two rules to think about. First, it doesn't matter if the audience can't see it properly – in fact it's half the fun and most of the point. Second: you should produce it from nowhere – preferably your pocket (that's my personal prop 'size limiter'). If you start your speech, and there is a small plastic bottle visible on the lectern or on the table in front of you, it's actually counterproductive. After two minutes, you will have lost the audience – they'll be trying to figure out what it is.

If you need more sophisticated visual aids, check out IDEA 30, *You can look at me or look at that...* and IDEA 32, *Come in, Houston.*

Try another idea...

I love this tactic. One key point I make in a lot of business speeches is the need to respect your customers – they hate being talked down to or patronised. In many hotel rooms there is now a little sign suggesting that, because of the world's water shortage and/or detergent pollution, it would be 'responsible' if you, the hotel customer, didn't want all your towels washed every day. This would be really powerful if they then added that, for every towel not washed, they would contribute one penny to irrigation projects. They don't. They just increase their operating margins, using eco-bollocks to get us to help them. When I see such a card, I produce it at my next speech as an example of a company insulting its customers – adding (in my speech) that where I do see such a card, I use all the towels, dry my hair on the curtains and clean my shoes on the bedspread.

'Example is always more efficacious than precept.'
SAMUEL JOHNSON

Defining idea...

How did it go?

Q **I have a working model, which is a very helpful way of demonstrating the effectiveness of a machine I talk about in my speeches. What's the best way of using this with an audience?**

A *I can't see how it works with more than ten people around a table. If you really need to do this as part of your speech with bigger audiences, you need to invest in sophisticated visual aids – probably video. I'm talking about small, low-tech props, produced from nowhere that help the audience get the point.*

Q **I like to refer to odd newspaper and magazine cuttings to support points in my speeches, but find it cumbersome to put them on slides and up on the screen. Can you just use them as 'props'?**

A *Yes, yes, yes – but don't try and read from them directly, you probably won't be able to see them clearly. Just wave one about and summarise or quote from memory the bits you want. The audience will get the point.*

30

You can look at me or look at that

The occasional, judicious use of an audio and/or visual aid can be rewarding for both the speaker and the audience.

The pursuit of these rewards, however, is fraught with danger. The risk is that you cease to be a speaker, and become a presenter.

As a lifetime Manchester City fan (yes, there are two soccer teams in Manchester), I look on most visual aids as I do Manchester United. In my mind, the world would be a better place without them – but I have to acknowledge that they do exist, that a lot of people actually like them and that, sometimes, they do a good job.

Now, the impact of the march of technology on the options now available to a speaker has been massive. Let's start by looking at the basic dos and don'ts of using any of them.

I started to form my own golden rules on this subject back in the early 1970s when the company that had the privilege of employing me sent me on a kind of outward-bound course. It was run by John Ridgway, who had recently completed the first

Here's an idea for you... **When you've planned and rehearsed your speech, and built in any appropriate visual aids you feel you need, have another run-through which includes a plan for a power failure. How will you compensate for suddenly being deprived of your AVs? How would you summarise them using only your voice and gestures? This does two things: first, in the unlikely event that the power does fail, you will not panic. Second: it will probably bring home to you that some of your AVs are better left out and handled by you as a speaker.**

transatlantic crossing in a rowing boat with Chay Blyth. The latter came to talk to us about it – and fairly quickly arrived at a slide showing a photo of his naked backside. It looked like something from the butchers. It had been taken about three days into the crossing, and graphically indicated the effect of rubbing your bum up and down a wooden seat as you rowed a boat for day after day. Later I asked him why he hadn't used a seat which moved with his backside, as they do in, for example, the Boat Race. His answer was that a seat which consisted of a wooden plank couldn't go wrong. If they had gone high-tech, and it had gone wrong in mid-Atlantic, they were in a much worse position than simply having sore arses.

I learned two universal laws about using visual aids from that half hour:

- The right picture can be worth a thousand words for the speaker and the audience. Chay Blyth could have tried to describe his raw bum, but (trust me) it would not have had the same effect. I can still see it now – thirty-odd yeas later.
- If you have a choice of technologies, plump for the lower-level one. There is less to go wrong – and, if it does, it's easier to improvise and carry on.

Before I get on to different types of audio/visual aids, I want to chisel in stone some of the implications and rules for using any or all of them.

Look in IDEA 25, *Can you tell what it is yet?*, for ideas on how you can use a simple chart pad instead of more sophisticated AVs.

Try another idea...

- Yes, they can be powerful and memorable, but they must only support you as a speaker – not the other way round. Do not use them just because you have them, or because they are cool. Use them to support and/or emphasise your key points.
- Using them will increase your reliance on extra facilities and/or extra people. These may range from the simple provision of more electrical sockets, to an assistant to work some equipment. Do not rely on any of these without personal verification.
- Many speakers use AVs (audio-visual aids) because they believe it adds to their professionalism. The converse is also true – do it badly and it makes you look amateurish.
- Using AVs puts much more pressure on rehearsal. Beforehand, you need to really familiarise yourself with whatever equipment is involved – so that its use is seamless and that you are its complete master. It also adds more pressure on the day – you need to test out all the equipment *in situ* so that you have complete confidence in and familiarity with it. Any audience will spot immediately if you are uncomfortable with the equipment.

Speak'er, n. One who speaks esp. in public.
Present, v.t.& i., & n. Exhibit thing to person.
Concise Oxford Dictionary

Defining idea...

131

How did it go?

Q **At the start of the speech, when you are 'telling 'em what you are going to say', does it make sense to put the key contents that you are going to cover on an AV?**

A *Short of going on stage with your zip undone or your skirt caught up at the back, I can't think of a dafter practice. The opening is a crucial stage for you to grip the audience, and anything approaching a 'list of contents' would be far better coming from your voice and through your gestures.*

Q **I am constantly being frustrated by venues being equipped with high-tech AV equipment, but when you arrive you find there is nobody who can work it or (quite frequently) perform the necessary part replacement or maintenance to get it up and running. Should I just abandon using it?**

A *No, you shouldn't, but this is the core problem. To manage this risk you must do two things: a) really familiarise yourself with the principles of any equipment you will be using, and b) bring what backup (e.g. disks) and spare parts (e.g. projector bulbs) that you can with you.*

31

Here's a picture of our new product upside down

'Physical' slides can be cheap, simple and effective tools in the speaker's armoury. There's not much to go wrong, really...

Apart, that is, from what you put on them.

35 mm slides or A4-sized acetates remain popular with speakers who struggle at home with the TV remote control. 35 mm slides are usually pre-packed into a carousel cartridge which is then locked into an overhead projector. The slides are then shown in sequence – a process which is triggered (usually) by a remote switch. Acetates are usually placed one-by-one on to the flat bed of a projector. The end result is the same – the enlarged contents of the slide appear, filling an appropriately sized screen which is visible to everybody in the audience.

The key to slide effectiveness is content and/or design – and here I would like to ask a simple question of all speakers: why on earth would you use a slide consisting only of words? I have seen thousands of these, and in every case my belief was that the whole process would have been better if the speaker had left the slide off and spoken the words. Audiences hear at the same rate, but they read at different speeds – so it's an uneasy minute or so while you, the speaker, judge whether it's time to move on. And just what do you do, as a speaker, while they are reading the contents?

Here's an idea for you...

The 35 mm carousel (particularly) is inflexible if you need to repeat a slide. If you plan to show a slide twice during a presentation, then produce it twice and put the second one in the correct place in the sequence.

Slides are about adding to words, not delivering them. They are best when providing a visual impact or explanation. It would have taken thousands – millions – of words to describe the impact of the Ethiopian famine in the 1980s, but a few pictures of the affected children got the world digging into its pockets. Have you ever tried to describe a pie chart? Go on, have a go. Come back when you've finished.

See what I mean?

Of course, you might have to use a few words on a slide – in which case, make them big, at least 1 cm tall on an A4 acetate slide. Use a clear font (like Times New Roman). Only print horizontally, even if it's a vertical graph index you are labelling, or an off-vertical segment of a chart. Use mixed upper and lower case; it's easier to read. If you want to highlight a word, use the same font but make it bold. Keep any colours clear and distinct (yellow looks like white from the back of the room).

The UK comedian Benny Hill once famously said: 'I know how to spell Antonioni, I just don't know when to stop.' This brings us to the big challenge with slides – trying to get too much content on each one. Apply the T-shirt Law – which states that, on the front of any T-shirt, you can only get one picture and/or message across to a largely disinterested audience. You should ruthlessly edit your slides for this, and if you need to get more content on a slide, and you overstep the T-shirt Law, put it on another, or a 'build-up' slide.

If you need to show a complex picture (e.g. an engineering drawing), pick out the bit you need to show to support your point, and either reproduce that on another slide, or highlight just that particular bit and blank off the rest. If you have columns of figures, ditto. In the world of slides, less is more.

If you are using an OHP (overhead projector), the room set-up becomes critical. For ideas on this, read IDEA 8, *The feng-shui factor*.

Try another idea...

Here's some advice for each specific mechanism:

- For 35 mm slides: if you are using a carousel, you should load it, seal it with tape personally, and then never let it out of your sight. Test it, and set it up in the start position when you get to the venue. You will need the lights dimmed for your show, so check out who will do that for you, and when.
- For overheads (acetates): you need to be very careful with the positioning of the projector – if you get it off-centre, or out-of-whack vertically, the resulting slide gets badly distorted on the screen – and bang goes your professionalism. Print your slides beforehand (don't try the fancy felt-tip-pen-real-slide-writing-time thing). Frame the acetates, otherwise they will curl. Bring a spare projector bulb and an extension lead with you.

'I know of only one rule: style cannot be too clear, too simple.'
STENDHAL, French author

Defining idea...

135

How did it go?

Q **I use 35 mm slides throughout my presentation, but always seem to be standing in the wrong place while they are on screen. If I try to highlight something on screen, I end up being the screen. Or I end up wrestling the remote slide switch and the microphone, and facing the wrong direction. Are there some simple technical things I could do to make this easier?**

A *There are two things you can't do. First, you shouldn't turn your back on the audience – so make sure your microphone will allow you to get away from the screen and stand sideways on. Second, you can't highlight something with your finger. Either make sure the slide design highlights the key point or image, or use a remote (e.g. laser) pointer to pick it out.*

Q **I understand you cannot leave a slide on when you've finished with it, but how do you avoid a white screen or the next slide appearing too soon?**

A *If there is a gap when a slide is 'finished' you have a number of alternatives. One way is simply to switch the machine off or use a lens cap. You can also fit blank (dark), or neutral (e.g. logo or title) slides into the carousel where a gap comes up.*

32

Come in, Houston

Armed with relatively cheap equipment, a solo speaker can now put on an audio-visual show that has a lot in common with a U2 concert.

The benefits are stunning, and still not fully understood or quantified. The drawback is that you can say the same about the downsides...

Cutting-edge technology offers the speaker the kind of opportunities that the internet offers the world. Now, a warning: I am to high-tech what the Osbournes are to smooth family functionalism. I spent many years examining Kleenex boxes to find the battery: hey, you pull one out, another one pops up – that needs a battery, trust me. But I have learned a lot about technology and speaking, and I have watched a lot of speakers wrestle with it. Most of them have not found their problems in preparation, but in the uneasy marriage of their technical bits with the host's technical bits. What happens when they don't match is usually funny – for the audience.

Here's an idea for you...

A lot of the advanced AVs are PC-based, and you may want to take your own laptop with you. That's discretionary, and depends on a) what you have been told about what's there and b) how much you trust it. What I would do, however, is buy yourself a hand-held or remote mouse, and bring it with you, along with appropriate software. This gives a speaker a sense of familiarity and flexibility – which is great for both confidence and professionalism.

Don't get me wrong here. I think Powerpoint is a magnificent tool when the (virtual) slides follow the T-shirt rule – one T-shirt, one message – and when they are used to add impact to the speaker's key messages. You can access almost infinite material – charts, spreadsheets, scanned pictures – and you can carry the lot (including full backup) around with you. It doesn't stop with Powerpoint: if an event organiser informs me that my walk-on music is to be Barry Manilow, I inform him that this will not be the case while he has a hole in his bum – and hand him my iPod. There is nearly four days' worth of musical material on it.

Advanced technology is not only a threat when it doesn't work, it can threaten to take over the speech. Its use or non-use has to be personalised to each speaker, but here are two examples which bring home my lessons. I witnessed two 'motivational' speakers within a few weeks of each other, and both were from the world of English rugby. One was a retired player, who will remain nameless; the other was Sir Clive Woodward, prior to his World Cup triumph. Here's what happened:

- The player went all high-tech, combining Powerpoint slides, which were all words, with a dozen or so video clips of him scoring tries. The words he spoke (when not reading out the slides' content) tried to knit all this together into motivational lessons for the assembled fruit-machine salesmen. The venue was a high-tech theatre, but the speaker's efforts in stopping and starting the video clips, going to and from the PC for his slides and intermittently blowing into his microphone to see if it was live, should have been filmed for all to see. He would have been better not turning up and phoning it in.

For further information on the T-shirt Law for slide design, try IDEA 31, *Here's a picture of our new product upside down.*

Try another idea...

■ Sir Clive also used Powerpoint – but about six slides in forty minutes. They looked professional and each one 'visually' banged home a key message. He wasn't (then) a natural orator, but his intensity combined with a few very carefully chosen and professionally designed visual aids provided a genuinely memorable combination.

Don't let technology take over either the performance or the content – and recognise that the more advanced it is the more chance there is of either or both these happening. If you use Powerpoint, get there early to check your software on their PC. Do this twice. Do not be tempted to make last minute changes. Don't get fancy – avoid the temptation of, for example, digital zooming. The *Blair Witch* approach to home video might have had its advantages for the filmmakers, but it will not impress many live audiences.

If you use video, I have two pieces of advice. First: it is expensive, but get it done professionally. Second: work with an assistant. Keep the clips short, and have somebody else in charge of starting and finishing them, controlling the lighting and managing what's on the screen in between.

Don't attempt to talk over a video clip – make your points before or afterwards.

'*The thing with high-tech is that you always end up using scissors.*'
DAVID HOCKNEY

Defining idea...

How did
it go?

Q **I am planning a speech, and want to use just a couple of visual aids. It seems an awful lot of extra effort and kit just to add this dimension to my speech. Should I just abandon the idea – or maybe add a few more slides?**

A *Stay with your plan. If your instinct is that just two visuals are needed, then just two it is. The whole point about technology for a speaker is that you should master its use (so it becomes effortless), but you should not become a slave to it.*

Q **I use an assistant, usually recruited on the day, to trigger my slides. I don't use many, but because I speak from a combination of memory and brief notes, it seems impossible to agree the 'cues' for the slides with the assistant beforehand and then get him or her to trigger them on the right cues. Do I have to do this myself (with a remote switch on stage) to make sure?**

A *Yes. The only way to guarantee a stranger will do the job you want is to provide them with what is virtually an annotated script, with the exact places where he or she presses the switch marked quite clearly in a pre-agreed way.*

33

I seem to have moved from 33 to 45 rpm

There are some – thankfully rare – occasions when a speaker must have control over the word-by-word content and/or exact timing of a speech. And that's where Autocue comes in...

The use of Autocue can <u>almost</u> guarantee the exact delivery of a planned script on a planned timescale. It can also almost guarantee a flat, uninspired performance.

Autocue technology enables the speaker to read from a visual aid (usually a screen), that he or she can see, but the audience can't. Autocue manifests itself in a number of technical forms, but they all have one thing in common. The script is written out, word for word, beforehand. It can be 'personalised' to help phrasing, emphasis and timing, but it must be typed out, virtually word for word, because it arrives on a screen in front of the speaker in letters that can be read.

By definition, the screen will, at any one time, contain only a few lines – and will therefore have to scroll forward as you progress through the speech. This means that somebody else will be controlling the scrolling speed, and herein lies a core problem. It is (I hope obviously) the Autocue operator's job to match your pace

Here's an idea for you...

In 1863, Abraham Lincoln delivered, at Gettysburg, one of history's great speeches. The first few lines are written below. Using codes, annotate it for Autocue delivery by you – with one addition. At the end of the first paragraph, plan to leave the script for an unscripted anecdote:

'Fellow countrymen, fourscore and seven years ago, our fathers brought forth on this continent a new nation, conceived in liberty and dedicated to the proposition that all men are created equal.

Now we are engaged in a great civil war, testing whether that nation – or any nation so conceived and so dedicated – can long endure. We are met on a great battlefield of that war. We have come to dedicate a portion of that field as a final resting-place for those who here gave their lives so that that nation might live. It is altogether fit and proper that we should do this.'

when scrolling your speech, and not the other way round. If you are not used to it, however, something strange happens. Because you are reading, you tend to speed up. The operator responds accordingly, and you the speaker, respond back – probably subconsciously – by speeding up more. The operator notices this… and you see where this is going? You end up speaking like one of the Chipmunks, or like one of your old 33 rpm records being played at 45 rpm.

There are tools and techniques to manage the Chipmunk Factor, but let's first put Autocue in its context. It is essential for people like newsreaders and party political broadcasters. If there's a lot of legal and/or technical stuff in your speech, it can be a real help. If you are making a video recording of a speech, you may want to trade off some of the 'live' magic to ensure you get your content and timing exactly right – and Autocue technology will allow the camera to film through the screen you are reading from so you can look straight into it. If you feel that someone may put parts of your upcoming speech under a microscope, and that any loose words might come back and bite you, then you might want to Autocue all or part of your talk. But for the vast majority of speaking occasions, particularly if you are an invited guest speaker, Autocue will not be appropriate for you, the audience or the venue.

If you need to read bits of your speech verbatim but won't or can't use Autocue, check out IDEA 23, *I'm sorry, I'll read that again*.

Try another idea…

If you do use it, you can annotate the script with your own 'codes' to help you manage timing, phrasing and emphasis. Always use double (line) spacing. Ordinary words are typed like this, but if you need some emphasis **type them in bold**. If you really want to pound a point home, then **type it in underlined bold**. I stay with just those three, but I also add marks for pauses. One ● in a script means I pause, leave the script, and look at the audience for two seconds; two of these ● ● means four seconds. Three of them mean a big dramatic pause, where I probably take a drink. If I want to leave the script completely for a couple of minutes (perhaps to tell an anecdote) I say so in the script *in a different font, with a note to the operator indicating at what point I will come off-script, and the exact point I will rejoin it.*

'Your weight is ten stone nine pounds.'
A typical comment emitted by an 'I speak your weight' machine – also the effect resulting from most speakers using Autocue…

Defining idea…

145

How did it go?

Q   I have only used Autocue once, but I felt very 'artificial' with my head fixed in one position for large parts of my delivery. Can you do anything to increase your flexibility with this technology?

A   *Depending on budgets and facilities, you can use two screens. If you, the speaker, are facing 'north' to your audience, you can position one screen at north-west and the other at north-east. The same script and scrolling occur on both screens, but this gives you a lot more flexibility for gestures and head movement if you move between the two. It can't be that difficult – George W. Bush uses two screens.*

Q   Can you use Autocue for just a 'tricky' part of your speech?

A   *It's a bit like having a Rolls-Royce as a backup car, but – if the budget runs to it – it's a failsafe way of guaranteeing the exact content when you need to.*

34

Dreading the wedding

There's one speaking challenge like no other.

I refer to making a speech at a formal family occasion — the most popular being a wedding...

Many people make their first and only public speech at a family wedding. It is an event. It has a speaker, (usually) a microphone and an audience – but, at a wedding, these mix together to produce something with an entirely different DNA structure to an ordinary public-speaking occasion.

Weddings are normally quite structured affairs, certainly until the speeches are over. There are also many documented 'common-sense' rules, some of which I will reprise here. What makes a wedding unique is that the structures and the rules are totally different from those for almost any other speaking occasion – and this has two primary consequences:

- An experienced speaker is not guaranteed to do well. The subject isn't about management, or products, or customers, or footballers – the subjects are two vulnerable, happy people that most of the audience have known for years. The delivery mode isn't about professionalism, it's about emotion. It's about heart, not head. The audience isn't a distant sea of blurry faces, they are recognisable relatives. This is a case where experience can work against you.

Here's an idea for you... **If you've got a wedding speech now inked firmly in your diary, start immediately to prepare it. Just dump down ideas (memories, stories, things you think you might be able to use from elsewhere, anecdotes that have made you laugh, etc.). Don't worry about having too much material and too little shape. A couple of weeks before the event, start to knead it and shape it into two or three stories. Pinch bits from here and bits from there to embellish them – and pretty soon you will have all you need.**

- An inexperienced speaker, however, can win the day. The audience are willing you to do well – and all the more so if they know you are a rookie. They don't want motivating, or to share information or to buy anything. They want a bit of entertainment and fun. There are tons and tons of material for you to draw on. About 90% of poems, songs and entertainment routines revolve around people – and that doesn't include stuff you can make up. This is the one speech you really don't have to worry about – so follow a few rules and enjoy yourself.

I'm not going to list a pile of wedding one-liners and the rules of who says what when. Type in 'wedding speeches' on an internet search engine, and you will be there all week with the results. But here are some dos and don'ts. They are mainly about avoiding pratfalls...

- Do check your duties. The main speeches at a wedding are toasts. If you are collared for one, understand the main purpose of yours – and what you do when you finish.
- Don't drink beforehand. This is not a big deal as there is usually plenty going on after the speeches – but standing up after a few jars is one sure-fire way to snatch defeat from the jaws of victory. You can do a lot of damage if you ignore this rule.

- Focus on the bride and groom. It's their day.
- Research the basics. A very good speech can go straight down a snake by mixing up Aunt Mildred and Aunty Betty. And verify things – how exactly do you pronounce Siobhan?
- Check (with both sides) of the family for sensitive areas. Every family has some, but some are more hidden than others. Having the bride's step-mother standing up and walking out half way through your speech is not conducive to a standing ovation.
- Don't score cheap points against some family member who has pissed you off for twenty years. It's not the time or place.
- Be careful with your comedy. Of course, part of the deal is to make the audience laugh. But remember, there may be three generations present, and whereas you hardly notice the 'f' word, you can be sure granny will. Don't try and work the family artificially into punchline jokes. Keep the humour light, clever and focused on the couple (although a couple of short anecdotes at your own expense will help your cause). Funny stories, with the relevant bits slightly exaggerated, work well.
- It is becoming popular, particularly in the US, to have an 'open microphone' at the end of the formal speeches – so that anybody present can offer their tribute to the happy couple. My advice? If you are not on the formal team sheet, give it a miss. On a scale of one to ten, I would score the potential upside of such a venture as about one, and the potential downside as about minus thirty.

Weddings often involve alcohol – and for more thoughts on speaking with lots of it around, read IDEA 26, *Ish a pleasure (hic) to be here.*

Try another idea...

'There are individual men and women, and there are families.'
MARGARET THATCHER

Defining idea...

149

Q   **I'm slated to be best man at my pal's wedding, and I have pinched a rather compromising (although not 'rude') picture of his bride-to-be from a few years back. I'm thinking of having copies made, and circulating them for a 'caption competition' during my speech. Will this upset anybody?**

A   *Are you nuts? Do everyone a favour – burn the photo.*

Q   **I'm concerned that a good part of the audience at an upcoming wedding speech I have to give will not know me. Will it cause offence if I'm overfamiliar with the bride and groom when half of the folk present will not know my relationship with them?**

A   *It's not a problem if you take a bit of time to explain how you fit in. For example, if you are best man, spend some time explaining your links to the groom and family. Once you stop being a stranger, you can get away with a lot more.*

35

Food, glorious food

A growing trend in this hurried world is for events to include 'working' meals.

The organisers will insist that the agenda continues while the meal is going on — and the guest speaker is usually the easiest to fit in this awkward slot.

For a speaker, the presence of food can have the same effect on a speech as static interference does on a broadcast. You can hear the content, but the additional noise dilutes its effectiveness. This interference needs to be minimised.

This annoying trend started with the so-called 'Big Bang' that affected anything (but particularly businesses) that purported to have cross-border interests. Everything was suddenly 24/7. At a stroke, the three-Martini lunch died in the US. In the UK, tragically, the great lunchtime conundrum was left unanswered: why is it that, at lunchtime, a half bottle of claret is OK for one, but a full bottle is never quite enough for two?

Here's an idea for you…

Decide now whether you are an eater or non-eater. If it is a meal-based speech, do you eat it with the audience – or do you get introduced, come on and do your stuff and then clear off? Each to their own, but my advice would be not to eat with the audience if you have the option. The first reason for that is selfish: I never want to eat just before a speech, and prefer a bit of solitude to get myself mentally set up. If you are introduced at the time of your speech, and they have not seen you before, I also think it helps to give you impact and to combat interference. My antisocial stance on this also prevents me giving my speech, in advance, over the meal, to the ten people around me. I also believe, however, that such a meal is a chance for the peer-group members of the audience to catch up and talk over their stuff without having to play host to a stranger who will be out of their lives in a couple of hours. (I then make up for this by mingling heavily after the speech, often until the bar shuts.)

Stress levels soared. Meetings and events became chaotic. Agendas expanded until they accounted for all non-sleeping hours, and many guest speakers were handed a brief which included the sad words: 'We're looking for a for a forty-minute slot on leadership, which will be in Ballroom A while lunch is being served.'

I'm leading the resistance. Here are my ideas.

The room set-up: Get your speaking position away from the table where the food is served. Even if the room is flat (i.e. has no stage) there will be a better place in it to give a speech to a dining audience than the one created by standing up where you have eaten, pushing your chair back and working with a hand-held or fixed microphone. You have no room for (physical) manoeuvre and some of the audience are going to be outside your field of vision unless you are a contortionist. The room set-up options for food service are usually variants of two basic models: either 'U' shaped rows and columns, or round tables with eight to ten people on each one. Find a spot where you can see all the audience, and base yourself there. If you can move from there during the speech, so much the better: if you can get within ten feet of the diners, you are much more likely to beat the dead chicken for their attention. The round table model is the best of all for this. What happens is that each table becomes a little community, with its own 'personality', during a meal – and if you can work this out pretty quickly you can play one off against another.

Then find a spot in the meal process which 'lends itself' to an activity pause – no waiters, no audience 'up and downing' and minimal chewing. With most served meals there is a spot where the main course has been cleared, and desserts and coffee have been served. You need to agree this with the catering manager and/or organisers beforehand, but try and start your speech then. If the organiser then pre-announces your speech (by, say, ten minutes) ensuring the audience can have a loo break before you start, and you agree with the catering person that no waiters will serve during your speech, you have minimal interference.

For more ideas on setting up the room the way you want it, try IDEA 8, *The feng-shui factor.*

Try another idea…

'A man seldom thinks with more earnestness of anything than he does of his dinner.'
SAMUEL JOHNSON

Defining idea…

How did it go?

Q **I was speaking at an event recently where we were all running late. It was suggested that people in the audience grabbed a plate of lunch and brought it back to the auditorium and ate while I spoke. It was a bit chaotic, and I was wondering if I should have refused to cooperate?**

A *I don't think so. This is different from a planned speech/meal combination – and you are helping all concerned to get back on track. The audience will recognise this, and be on your side. You can also have a bit of fun in this kind of situation ('You will notice that I keep moving about when I talk... I only do this in front of an audience equipped with aerodynamic chunks of garlic bread...').*

Q **What's the best way to convince a reluctant catering manager to rearrange his serving schedule to accommodate the pauses and delays you want?**

A *If you are speaking at a catering-based function, take a small amount of cash with you – a couple of low-denomination notes. They go a long way to getting what you want – and (if you are a non-eater but clever) a plate of food and a glass or two kept back for after your speech.*

36

As I am sure you will have read in *The Economist...*

Gain the respect of the audience by becoming a hunter-gatherer of bits and pieces of information ('stuff') that adds wit, relevance, alertness, breadth and credibility to your strength or specialism.

Imparting specialist knowledge on your chosen subject(s) is not, in itself, enough...

Speakers lose the respect of an audience if they show themselves to be out of touch with the world outside. Silly mistakes, obvious areas of not-done homework and poor awareness of the audience's world can send even the most expert specialist speaker sliding down a snake.

This is not about getting properly briefed for a speech, or researching your own subject. This is about the good speaker's constant trawl for material that supports and/or illuminates the keynote messages of the speech. It may come from unlikely sources, and take unlikely forms, but its use must obey an important rule. It doesn't matter whether it is a fundamental point of the speech, an entertaining throwaway line, a reference to the world outside or an anecdotal ramble – if it contains information that is in the public domain, it has to be right.

Here's an idea for you...

Start now. Grab a piece of paper, and for the next twenty-four hours jot down (or steal) any bits of information that catch your eye that you think you might just use in a speech. As an example here's mine. They're not grammatical, and they have no direct relevance to any of my speaking 'subjects' – but they'll go in the databank and I'll use them somehow, some day:

- **America: land of wide open spaces. Usually surrounded by teeth.**
- **Every day another species becomes extinct. Every day, another Starbucks opens.**
- **'Duckau' and 'Mausevitz' – staff names for EuroDisney**
- **When the music stops, they add a chair.**
- **His desk was so big it had its own zip code.**
- **'I am told that a horseshoe brings you luck whether you believe it or not.' (Nils Bohr)**

Somewhere, in the previous paragraph, is the word 'constant' – and that's the key to this idea. Almost everything a regular public speaker sees or hears in everyday life passes through a kind of mental filter. This complex process takes a nano-second, and involves two questions being asked – is what I have just seen or heard memorable, and if so, can I use it in my speeches?

Speakers are avid jotters and hoarders. They are always writing down bits of stuff (usually, in my case, on the back of my hand with a biro). At the end of the day, their pockets will be full of bits torn out of newspapers or magazines. If they read a novel, they are figuring out how they can use a bit of background information or a turn of phrase. If they are watching sport on TV, they are working out if they can use some analogies or examples to support their own specialist subject. If anything – anything – makes them smile, they'll remember it and try it out sometime to see if it gets the same response from an audience. And they all have a notebook by their bedside.

All this stuff can – and should – go down in your own data bank, and this is one area where the PC has made life so much easier. I have one file headed 'Stuff', which is now a dozen, closely typed, pages long. I have another file where I keep scanned stuff. When I've figured out the backbone and key segments of a speech, I'll then think about the audience and the setting – and then scroll through this lot for the 'decorative' supporting material. It never fails me.

> **For ideas on making sure the core content of your speech is relevant and factual, look up IDEA 4, *Brief encounters*.**

Try another idea...

I confess I remain a fan of the printed word. I know I could sit for an hour surfing the web and probably find all these nuggets and more, but I much prefer surfing papers, magazines and books. In the UK I subscribe to *The Economist*, the *Spectator*, *Business Week* and *Private Eye*. When I'm in the US, I add the *Onion*, *People Magazine* and *Entertainment Weekly*. If I'm travelling, it's the *New Statesman*, *Time* and *Newsweek*. If I could only access one of those, it would be *The Economist* – for a wonderful summary of what's going on the world, written in good English with the odd bit of humour. And no, I'm not getting paid for that endorsement.

> **'All generalisations are dangerous, even this one.'**
> ALEXANDRE DUMAS

Defining idea...

How did it go?

Q   If you are referring to information in the public domain, should you always quote your sources?

A   *There's a judgement call here. If you are quoting somebody, or you are assertively using facts to back up a key point, then you should state your sources clearly. If you are having a bit of fun to make a point 'live' – I discovered, for example, that if you stacked up $1 billion in single dollar bills, the pile would be seventy miles high – then just leave it hanging in the air. The point is not the actual height of the stack, but that a billion is a lot.*

Q   Is it right to refer to living people as examples of a point you are trying to make, without their permission?

A   *If it's a positive reference, and the information used is in the public domain, then it's not only OK, it's a very useful tool. I use a couple of long-lived entertainers as examples of constant personal reinvention when I'm talking to business leaders. If you're looking for negatives, however, you need to be a lot more careful. You could upset parts of your audience – and there are laws against slander.*

37

Unaccustomed as I am

An effective public speaker is one who has mastered, perhaps unknowingly, some of the many varieties of modern rhetoric.

These help to persuade an audience to accept both the speaker and the speech.

The main goals of a speech centre around one of these, or a combination of them:

a) To sell something (e.g. products, services, ideas).
b) To pass on information.
c) To motivate or inspire.

Common to any or all of them is the need to entertain – and to convince the audience of your credibility and of your content's integrity.

I'm not talking about something new here. Rhetoric was a hot subject with the ancient Greeks, and Aristotle wrote a book on it sometime around 300 BC. He defined rhetoric as the means of persuasion, and its importance in the history of democracy – where persuasion supposedly took over from force as a means of making your case – cannot be overstressed. Aristotle identified three means of persuasion:

■ *Ethos*: persuasion through force of character.
■ *Pathos*: persuasion through the arousal of emotion.
■ *Logos*: persuasion through logic.

Here's an idea for you...

Take one of your existing speech 'segments', and, if you haven't got one, pick one story from the TV news tonight. Then rewrite whichever it is, as part of an upcoming speech you are to give – but with a couple of added dimensions. Illustrate the key point(s) by the use of figurative language or verbal imagery in two ways. First, in a way that will make the audience smile and, second, the same point, but this time in a way that will give them a gentle shock. You have just paddled into the shallow waters of rhetoric.

Modern rhetoric is almost unrecognisable from its ancestors, but those categories still broadly cover the techniques. It is the second one, however – persuasion by the arousal of emotion – that has grown at the expense of the others, and dominates the use (and abuse) of rhetoric today. There will be a few of you who, by now, will be muttering that I've lost the plot, and that this rambling pile of bollocks has nothing to do with your immediate challenge to give a speech at your company's next regional meeting. It is difficult without going into pages of quasi-science and lots of Latin, but it is important that the basic ideas come alive for you because modern audiences are exposed to bucketfuls of rhetoric every day.

Andrew Marr, the BBC's political correspondent, wrote recently about his 'trade' – journalism. One of the changes he has noted in his time in it has been the move from just passing on information to the receiving audience, to the 'reshaping' of that information so that it evokes an emotional response in the viewer or listener. The news isn't that three soldiers died today in Iraq; the news is that one of them was about to be married, and here is a film of the weeping bride-never-to-be. An expensive watch isn't advertised as a great time-keeper, it is advertised with the line that you never 'buy' this brand of watch, you look after it for the next generation. Charities compete – literally – by producing even more shocking images of the suffering they work to alleviate. The government leaks information that plays on the fear of terrorism the day before it announces another security initiative.

Now, you want laughter, fear, shock or mystification, and to those four I would also add sympathy, admiration and enlightenment. It's the science (or art) of using your language, sound and body to trigger emotions in an audience that make them more responsive to you and your speech. Add to that a couple of teaspoons of Aristotle's other classes of rhetoric (the powers of character and logic) and here are some of the basic techniques:

- Diminution: I'll start with the famous one ('Unaccustomed as I am...') as an example whereby you drop veiled hints that you are not (for reasons usually beyond your control) up to this speaking task. Target: audience sympathy.
- Figurative language: using memorable metaphors, similes and verbal imagery to support your key points. Make them laugh, make them cry, make them afraid, shock them, whatever supports your position – but make them feel something.
- Climax: building up through several platforms of reasoning, often using part repetition, to a strong, finishing key point.
- Repetition: much evidenced in modern public life by the use of sound bites, the drip-feeding of a key idea into the memory of an audience.
- Word sounds: onomatopoeia and alliteration – making words or groups of words stick in the memory via the impact of their sound.
- Hyperbole: exaggeration to increase an effect.
- Rhetorical questions: those that don't require an answer, but are positioned to bring focus on a subject so that you can answer it.

'*A good storyteller shapes and performs his/her narrative... to elicit the desired response, be it laughter, fear, shock or mystification.*'
SIMON FEATHERSTONE, 'Everyday Rhetorics' in *Speaking Your Mind*

Defining idea...

For specific ways of making an audience laugh, look up IDEA 16, *Laugh, I thought I'd never start.*

Try another idea...

How did
it go?

Q   **Is it risky to use sarcasm as a way of getting an audience to feel good by laughing at itself?**

A   *I have witnessed a couple of speakers who regularly have a dig at the audience ('I hear NASA used to train in this room. No atmosphere') but have never felt its potential benefits outweighed its risks. As a tool of audience 'persuasion' I can only see it convincing them that you're a clever dick, and there's a big risk of alienation there.*

Q   **Are there some individual words that are less threatening/more persuasive than others?**

A   *There are – and the list is almost infinite. For example, a salesman doesn't talk about you 'buying' something, but 'owning' it – and they generally find alternatives to 'cost', 'signing', 'minimum' and 'contractual'. In the same way, you should put your proposed key points under a microscope, and play around in your thesaurus with some of the important words. Some alternatives will do the job better than others.*

38

Does my bum look big on that?

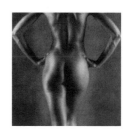

Speakers are increasingly finding video recording equipment present at events.

Video, whether broadcast simultaneously on big screens in big venues, or at a later date for memories and/or reference, is a cruel medium. It flatters only supermodels.

Let's first deal with a protocol issue. As a speaker, you have every right to be annoyed if you arrive at a venue and find a video camera trained on the stage if there has been no prior notification. It is more than just a matter of courtesy. If you are a celebrity, you will not want a pirate DVD competing with your official one next Christmas – but any speaker should want to control the quality and distribution of any performance recordings. Some speakers will simply refuse to allow any further use of such a recording, others are happy if it is just used internally by the host organisation. Two rules should apply, however:

- You must agree beforehand that a recording can be made – and also agree any future use of it.
- Always, always insist on seeing and approving a copy before they do anything with it.

Here's an idea for you...

If you know in advance that a speech of yours is to be recorded, and you do not have a video of a previous one, buy yourself a cheap camcorder and get somebody to train it on you for a few minutes, zooming in and out from full figure to facial close-up. Check out your favourite stance and gestures. If you are squeezing into a tight shirt collar, for example, accept the truth and go and buy one an inch bigger. Watch out for any nervous gestures (running your hand through your hair, scratching your nose, etc.).

Why would anyone want to video you? One reason is to do with the size and/or position of the audience. The trend is towards 'bigger, better, fewer' events, and you may find yourself facing a huge audience – particularly if you are tucked under a big celebrity keynote speaker. I found myself warming up a 15,000-strong, live, indoor audience for Christopher Reeve in Los Angeles, and (frankly) I couldn't see the back of the crowd. The only way they could see me was via a bunch of huge video screens, strategically placed, high above the auditorium. It's now commonplace at much smaller events than this. Another reason to video a speech is to allow the host organisation to have a record of the event, so they can share it with other people who weren't present.

Once you have agreed, and the video recording light goes on, your problems start. Unless it is an intimate (less than twenty) audience set-up, a male speaker will not – under normal circumstances – have to worry about whether or not he has trimmed his nose hair. Apart from making you look like an elephant, video highlights exactly that kind of gem...

Assuming you can't lose ten pounds before your speech, there are things you can do to offset the cruelty of this medium:

For more ideas on appearance and image, check out IDEA 11, *Speaker flies undone.*

Try another idea...

- Wear clothes that help the cause: dark colours work best – and if you have to have lines make them vertical (stripes) and not horizontal (hoops). Narrow stripes or checks (e.g. on a shirt or blouse) don't work. Avoid shiny accessories.
- Really, really, check your close-up appearance before you go on. If it's a professional production job, and the whole thing is being recorded, they may well have somebody who will appear with a make-up kit. Men may blanch at the thought, but in these circumstances this person is a friend. This medium really is cruel in close-up (particularly if it's a twenty-foot-tall close-up), and shiny noses and/or sweaty upper lips can prove surprisingly negative. Some men may have to shave again before appearing on video.

'Look at the size of my arse on that!'
BARRY GIBBONS, Los Angeles Convention Center

Defining idea...

These are not vain or frivolous ideas. The camera picks up every facial movement, and you must remember that the recording will probably be replayed in a smaller, more intimate room, without the magic of a live atmosphere.

'Well, you're not exactly fucking Kylie.'
(ENGLISH) VIDEO CAMERAMAN, same venue

...and another...

How did it go?

Q **I had a speech recorded on video recently, and was quite pleased with the result – with one exception. When viewed on a VCR I seemed quite serious – almost unfriendly – even for my lighter bits, and even though I felt it went down well as a live speech. How can I get 'warmer' for small video audiences?**

A *If you know that you will be recorded for future use, this is the stuff you need to practise. A video audience will see your performance on a one-to-one basis, and you need to adjust your delivery to reflect both the needs of the excitable live audience and the more intimate future one. A simple answer is to soften your face and smile more.*

Q **I saw part of a speech of mine which had been included in an edited video of the whole event. Everything had been shortened, but I felt that the editor cut my key messages and lost the thread of my arguments. Is the only way to combat this to insist on a complete editorial veto?**

A *If you agree to a video for 'internal' distribution, you are going to have to accept that you may be edited – and edited by someone who doesn't really understand your content. It's not a big deal. Just make sure you look OK, smile a lot and get your main points over. Do insist on seeing a copy before they do anything with it, but that's more about making sure any gaffes you made don't reach a wider audience.*

39

What's *really* important here is...

You may have to perform without the aphrodisiac of an audience...

These occasions involve performing solo, or being interviewed, in front of a camera in a studio setting.

The artificiality of a studio, coupled with the twin dangers of an interviewer and an editor who have different goals, can leave you remembered only for an unnaturally stilted performance and for something you didn't mean to say.

If you become known as a speaker, these occasions will arise with increasing frequency. This is different from having a speech recorded; this involves the deliberate use of a studio. The occasion could be anything from a message recorded for an event from which you are forced to be absent, to an internal training video for an organisation. Or it may be an organisational announcement for external distribution, which increasingly includes a ready-for-electronic-media element. Whatever the purpose, there are two categories: friendly and combative.

Here's an idea for you...

If you have an upcoming media interview, review your material with two things in mind. The first is: if I could only get one point across, what would it be? Then work on tactics (e.g. language, timing, repetition) to make sure you achieve that. Secondly, you should test how robust this point is for misinterpretation and/or twisting – and make tactical changes if there is a vulnerability.

The friendly occasion is where you are solo, or being interviewed by someone (essentially) on the same payroll. You are in charge of the process and content. Most, if not all, of the latter is scripted – and any questions asked are TV-chat-show type, gentle lobs thrown up into the air for you to bat down. There are no surprises, and I'm not going to spend much time on this, but I will add that a well-rehearsed use of Autocue can pay dividends here.

Let's now deal with the combative situation, where a speaker is faced with an interviewer and editor who control the process and content. To digest news and public-domain information today is like trying to drink from a fire hose. There is just so much of it, which brings two problems to the doors of presenters and editors. First, they have to get a thousand quarts into a pint pot, and edit down the (almost) infinite material available to them. Second, they have to compete against all the other media vehicles trying to bring their versions. In summary, they need to be short and newsworthy. If you are interviewed for a two-minute media slot, you will probably do a ten-minute interview. You, as a committed communicator, will assume that they will polarise to your key messages on your heartfelt positions. You will be wrong. Without any malice, they will first of all examine the material to see if you've pissed on your own shoes. Failing that, they will seek emotive potential in your content – drama, excitement, controversy. This is a more frightening challenge for a speaker than standing in front of an unknown audience. The challenge becomes one of avoiding negatives rather than accentuating the positives.

For more ideas on performing with Autocue, read IDEA 33, *I seem to have moved from 33 to 45 rpm.*

Try another idea...

Here are some dos and don'ts to protect your interests:

- Watch your phrasing and language. Remember Margaret Thatcher's 'There's no such thing as society'? It was taken entirely out of context, and is an example of how you really need to examine your use of language in advance, particularly on your key points. Can it be turned, twisted, misconstrued? If it can, it probably will be, so change it.

- You can, to a point, influence (or even control) the interview. The most blatant examples of this are to be heard on radio news programmes, generally in the morning, where politicians are often confronted for their views on overnight developments. If they are faced with a tricky question, they will invariably start their response by saying something like: 'That's an interesting point, but what's really important here is...' and then get their point over. You can also gain some control by remembering what the interviewer's success criteria are, and feeding them. If you use your best figurative language to support your points and repeat your sound bites, there's a chance your desired stuff will make the cut. Make sure you summarise strongly at the end (and that you have the last word if it's a debate). A lazy editor will probably use that sort of thing.

'An editor is one who separates the wheat from the chaff and prints the chaff.'
ADLAI STEPHENSON

Defining idea...

- Stick up for yourself. We've almost come full circle. The olden (golden) days of interviewer reverence have long disappeared, but there is more widespread acceptance now that interviewees can politely hold their own. If something you say is echoed back by an interviewer in a twisted way, then it is perfectly feasible to stop and insist that this is not what you meant. If you are interrupted, then ask politely to be allowed to finish your point.
- Don't bluff. I cannot pass on better advice on this subject than that given by Donald Rumsfeld: 'Learn to say "I don't know". If used when appropriate, it will be often.'

How did it go?

Q   However well I prepare, I find myself hurried by interviewers. This throws me off balance. How can I slow the process down?

A   The normal tactic for a speaker – the dramatic pause – is not available in this medium for the simple reason that the interviewer will fill it with another question! The key is to control the pacing of your voice (and breathing) during responses. Remember an interviewer is normally hurried (with a lot of other things to think about), but you needn't be.

Q   Can you take notes with you into a media interview?

A   I would strongly advise against it, even on radio. Most of these things are short, and the absolute key to you 'holding your own' is to be seen to be in control of yourself and your material.

40

'As God once said, and I think quite rightly...'

A common objective of any speech is to entertain – which is rarely achieved without humour. But here are the dos and don'ts of including religion and politics in your witty asides.

As a successful speaker you should also be aware of the world outside your speciality, so the idea that you should exclude all references to religion and politics serves nobody well.

I am writing this bit with a deafening row going on in the background. It is the international debate as to how much the post 9/11 world must trade-off personal liberty in order to sandbag our lives against the threat of terror. Legislation is rushing through assorted democratic assemblies to inhibit and/or prohibit offending anything or anybody. Public speakers are removing all material that hints at religion and/or politics. I'm not.

The key, of course, is to entertain the whole audience with your material, and not to offend part of it, or set one bit of it against the other.

Here's an idea for you...

Give yourself seven days, and trawl as much news media as you can in that time. Find two items (stories, quotes, pictures, whatever) from the worlds of politics and religion, that you would categorise as wonderfully daft. Take them as raw material, and then 'work' them into funny stories, anecdotes or references so that they can be used in your speeches. Ditch some bits, emphasise others. Cut and paste. Exaggerate. Add a small amount of made-up stuff. Do what you have to do.

Yes, think about any no-go areas, but unless you are addressing a group of born-again Christians, or a gaggle of neo-cons, there is a wealth of material you can use from politics and religion. Just remember that your material should be:

- Light and fluffy, not heavy and intense.
- Inclusive rather than alienating.
- Genuinely funny.
- Benign, if it's personal.

Here's an example: If you want to make a point about self-confidence and sure-footedness in any walk of life, then use the title of this idea. The British Field Marshall Montgomery, on one of his tours of the North African front during the Second World War, apparently drew up his jeep, clambered on the bonnet and, part way through his speech, uttered the immortal words: 'As God once said, and I think quite rightly...' and then carried on with his point. It's magnificent. If you want an example of a leader exuding confidence to men who needed confidence, faith and leadership – well, it's hard to better it. It is also wonderfully daft – once you realise you've heard it correctly you can't help laughing. And it's secular enough to be inoffensive to listeners from any religion.

Another example: Apparently, traditional toilet paper is being made obsolete in the US by the growth of a product called (I'm not making this up) Moist Wipes. Now, I heard a speaker address an American audience, and start by mentioning that fact. He then went on to say that he was a deeply religious man, and that the only comment he would make on this step forward in the ascent of man was that, the night previously, when he had

For more information on identifying real no-go areas, try IDEA 15, *A funny thing happened on the way to the crematorium.*

Try another idea...

been jotting down notes for his speech, he had difficulty even writing down the words 'Moist Wipes'. Again, it's gorgeous material for a speaker. You can use it to illustrate a bunch of points, the mental picture it creates is genuinely funny, and it's impossible to be offended.

If I'm in the US, I often use a routine which comments on their politics. You can't have a go at George Bush, because that gets heavy and divisive – but you can poke a bit of fun at Arnold Schwarzenegger, whoever is in the room: 'I left you all in charge of California – the world's fifth biggest economy – when I went back to live in England. And what happens? Who do you put in charge of it?' Republicans laugh because they think the idea is positively funny, and the Democrats join in because they think it's negatively funny.

I do believe that a public speaker should not sail against the wind of political correctness, and that remains my position. It may not represent your personal view (and it doesn't represent mine), but it's just not worth it; people who get upset by this stuff are now in every audience. But there are a million tons of material, in the worlds of politics and religion, that you can use without giving offence to anybody – and which offer up genuinely funny and/or entertaining stuff.

'Religion is a fine idea, if it wasn't for all that God stuff.'
'BARGEPOLE', *Punch* magazine

Defining idea...

How did it go?

Q   Is it OK to use personal examples from the world of politics or religion to illustrate a point in your speech?

A   *If you do mention personalities, you have to be very careful that you do not divide the audience. George W. Bush is somebody you either love or hate, and it is very difficult to use him (despite the wealth of material he chucks up) unless you know that all your audience is in one camp or the other. It's a good rule, however, to stay benign when referring to specific personalities – otherwise it easily crosses the 'offensive' line.*

Q   How can I be sure I am not guilty of slander when I use public names as negative examples in my speeches?

A   *This is really important, so photocopy it and keep it handy. You slander somebody if you say something about them that is untrue, and with the intent to harm their reputation. All the words are important in that sentence, but particularly the word 'untrue'. Many slander cases are lost because the slanderer got the facts wrong, not because there was any intention of harming someone's reputation. If you are referring to a person, check your facts twice – and if in doubt, leave it out.*

41

Uh-oh!

Public speaking is fraught with 'oh-no' moments – those magic times when you realise that, despite all your pre-planning and double checking, something has just gone seriously wrong.

Your consternation is added to by the scuttle of rats (e.g. organisers, producers, MCs, etc.) abandoning your sinking ship...

But it is this very loneliness that is the key to turning these situations into winning (and memorable) performances.

These oh-nos fall into two broad categories, and I've experienced them both. The most common is that the microphone and/or sound system fails – fully or in part (in my experience the latter is the more difficult challenge). A second favourite is where the human or technical assistance you need to show your visual aids falls down – and you and the audience are left looking at a white screen.

All of these can be turned from defeat into victory, but doing this needs a two-part mindset which will come a lot easier to a veteran speaker than it will to a rookie. The first part is the hardest – which is to stay calm. You are going to have to think

Here's an idea for you...

It's worth practising being naturally louder, just in case a system does go down on you. Because modern sound systems are so good, we tend to underuse our natural voice's power potential. Apparently, Demosthenes, in ancient Greece, practised his oratory against the sound of the beach surf so that he could be heard by large crowds – but if you walk up and down the beach yelling to yourself you'll get arrested today. However, you can and should practise if you can find a quiet spot. You will discover the difference between shouting and projecting. One is about screeching, and the other is about breathing, enunciating and pacing.

on your feet and take control, and you will do neither if you are frothing at the mouth.

The second part of the mindset is equally important, in that it helps the first. Repeat this to yourself: the audience is on my side. Remember, until you convince them otherwise, they are full of admiration for you for doing something that would terrify them – standing up in front of an audience. If life suddenly becomes (visibly) harder for you, you are banking even more goodwill. This is a wonderful weapon to have available in these circumstances. Have no shame – use it.

If your sound system fails, you are left with nature. If you are facing an audience of 15,000 there's little you can do, but for the vast majority of events, it will amaze you – and the audience – what a combination of your vocal chords, a re-jigged room and enhanced goodwill can achieve. Your first move is to make sure they all know what's happened (and, preferably, that it's not your fault). You turn this from a 'you' and 'them' situation to an 'us'

('Hey, folks: I'm here, you're all here – we're not going to let this beat us.'). Then, take a few minutes to look at your room set-up options. If you are on a stage, get off it. See if you can get down amongst the audience, and do something daft like stand on a chair. Turn it into pantomime season. Make some jokes. Get the people in the back rows to move forward if there's enough room at the front. Move about (with your chair), find different spots and change the angles. Increase your energy, gestures and decibels from your normal levels. Pick some faces out near the back, and talk (loudly) to them. You'll be able to tell if they can hear by their response. Just give it your best shot and you may well get a better reception than you would have done normally. In which case, think about using a microphone less.

If you use visual aids that require technology and/or assistance, you should plan on something going wrong. Rehearse summarising your slides' content verbally – and take hard copies with you if possible. Again, if it all goes pear-shaped, make sure the audience know what's happened – and then verbally improvise. As a by-product, I'm willing to place a small bet here: if this happens to you, you will use fewer visual aids in future.

For more ideas on (verbal) pacing and breathing, try IDEA 13: *Another opening, another show.*

Try another idea…

'Don't panic, Captain Mainwaring. Don't panic…'
CORPORAL JONES, in *Dad's Army*, classic BBC comedy series

Defining idea…

Q **What can you do if an 'oh no' is your fault – for example, you suddenly realise that you have misjudged your audience and/or material?**

A *One thing changes. You must still not panic, and you must still think on your feet – but you will attempt both of these without the added audience goodwill factor. It makes it harder, but not impossible. You should have your main material in self-contained segments, and be able to switch some out and some in while you are on your feet. It also helps if you have accumulated a library of alternative anecdotes, references, examples and stories that you can draw on to change the content and/or the style of a speech.*

Q **What happens if you suddenly realise that you have missed out a chunk of your speech? Should you go back and try and work it back in?**

A *No. Not unless it is the whole point of the speech. It comes as a bit of a blow to a speaker's ego – but it is a fact that most audiences won't realise a chunk has gone AWOL. It's gone, it's history. Don't muddle yourself even more, and confuse the audience, by trying to recover the fumble. Just press on, and make a mental note: you owe yourself and the audience a really good finish.*

42

And so, in conclusion...

There is wide disagreement among speakers, and those who write about speaking (who are not necessarily the same people), about how you should end a speech.

There is little disagreement, however, about the fact that it is the most important part of your performance.

The last minutes of your speech will define what your audience remembers about you and your material. However well or badly your speech has gone down, the ending represents an opportunity for a speaker to print some positive images in the audience's memory bank. If it's gone well, it's a chance to reinforce your success. If it's not gone well, it's a one-off opportunity to recover. The debate centres around how you structure the ending to achieve this impact – and it does need thought and planning.

Let's get rid of the extremists' views quickly. Propped up on my desk is a serious tome on speaking that proposes a long (and winding) road to a speech conclusion. The ending (it says) should include a summary of the salient facts and arguments, a reprise of key slides, proposals for future recommendations and actions, a list or description of references, any handouts, a thank you for patience and an invitation

Here's an idea for you...

Develop two alternative finishes for your normal speech. For each ending, work backwards from the last word of the last line. That should be a word that triggers your best laugh of the speech. That word may end a story, or an anecdote, or a one-liner or a punchline – but the chosen two need to be your two best. Then, if you use note cards, put the two finishes on differently coloured cards from the rest of the speech. When you've picked the most appropriate one for the day, you can move to it easily from different parts of your speech if you need or decide to go to the finish from an earlier part.

to ask questions. In my view, that not an ending, that's a siege. If I were in the audience, I would want an ice cream half way through it. At the other end of the debate are those who advocate that you should make your final point a good one, then simply shove a verbal full stop down, say 'thank you' and sod off. That's not an ending, that's an emergency stop. And, I think, a missed opportunity.

Here are my ideas:

■ Think of the word 'finish' as a noun. A finish needs to be part of your speech content in its own right. It needs planning, and it needs a teaspoon of your best material. The finish should follow your strongest key point.

■ Everything should be positive and confident in the finish. Avoid apologies ('Sorry I took so long'); avoid wishy-washy stuff ('I think that's about it').

■ It should include a summary of the key points and/or proposals you made. This does not involve going back over visual aids or redoing chunks of your speech, but a pithy, sound-bite-infested, punchy summary of no more than a handful of key points. It is a chance to reach back briefly to your opening objectives and, if you do it right, it will be the third repetition of the points you want your audience to think about and remember.

For some more ideas on structuring a speech, try IDEA 14: *One step at a time.*

Try another idea...

■ Give the audience a 'heads-up' that you are starting the finish. At the end of your last key point, use a link-in line (e.g. 'I must wind up in a couple of minutes so you can all use the loo before they lock up...') and get into it – probably via the summary. This heads-up does two things. For those who haven't been enjoying your speech (can you believe that?), it will at least make them alert and attentive again – and give you a last chance to win them over. Those who have been enjoying it (that's more like it) will want to savour the last few words – and they will be even more receptive to a memorable finish.

■ Unless you are a fourteen-carat grump, I suggest you use humour in and around your exit line. In my experience – both of my own audiences and of watching others – there is no better way of putting the final full stop to a speech than to generate a belly laugh in those listening. If you then add a simple 'thank you' it is almost automatic that the laugh will morph into applause, and in my experience the levels of both are correlated.

'A speech is like a love affair. Any fool can start it, but to end it requires great skill.'
LORD MANCROFT, British politician and writer

Defining idea...

How did it go?

Q **If you do feel it's right to state your sources and/or references, but don't want to clutter up your finish, how can you do that?**

A   *I would not do this verbally. If it's a list for further reading or future reference by the audience, have it typed up and copied. When the applause has peaked, either you or the MC can make the simple announcement that, for those interested, a copy is available on the way out.*

Q **A couple of times I have finished a speech, thankfully to good applause, but then lost some impact by nobody knowing what should happen next. There's a kind of vacuum. Is it my job to fill it?**

A   *It's not your responsibility, but it is your own fault if you allow defeat to be snatched from the jaws of victory this way. You should not start a speech without a clear understanding about what happens at the end. If you are on a stage, you want to leave it before the applause peaks. If you are working with an organiser, an MC or an introducer, you want agreement that they (or a 'voice of God' over the sound system) will acknowledge your speech and tell the audience what happens next.*

43

Over now to the Russian judge

In order to improve as a speaker you need to make yourself receptive to criticism.

There is an element of the 'ham' in all speakers, and a self-confidence that occasionally meanders towards vanity.

These, in the right amounts, are important characteristics for the sure-footed speaker. But all speakers need a process of continual small improvement to develop to their full potential. The Japanese call this *kaizan*, and it involves actively seeking constructive criticism as part of the self-improving process. Strangely enough, great speakers have great listening skills as well as great talking skills.

There is no more intoxicating sound to a speaker than the sound of hearty applause at the end of a speech. What is not so obvious to a happy and relieved speaker is that the same level of applause can mean different things, for example:

- Great speech! Wow, I really enjoyed that!
- WooWooWoo (this is a strange noise emitted by American audiences only, which means roughly the same thing).

Here's an idea for you...

In your pre-speech discussion with the organisers, ask if there will be any formal feedback or attitude survey after your speech. If there is, ask if you can get a copy in advance; simply say that you are keen to structure your speech against any formal success criteria designed for the event. This will give you some idea of what the organisers are looking for, which might be a help in shaping both your content and style.

However, the *same* applause can also mean:

- Thank heavens that's over. That was excruciating. Phew, it's finished.
- Eh? What? Oh – sorry, I dozed off. Is it finished? Great, I can go check my voicemail.
- Bar's open.

It is essential that you pick up the signals that the last three are different responses given via the same physical action – and learn why. I have been speaking in public – professionally – for a dozen or so years, and it is almost as though I am a different person from the one who started. Apart from looking vaguely the same, everything is different, and there was no big revolution involved. There was a lot of reflection, looking back on performances and banking my feelings on what worked and what didn't. There was a lot of trial and error. And there was a lot of listening to formal and informal feedback. As a result, no two speeches were the same – and the total change over a decade has been profound.

As a speaker today, you are helped by the 'attitude survey' culture that pervades modern life. Audiences are now routinely asked to fill in questionnaires about speeches, particularly if there is a paid speaker involved. This is neither the place nor the time to analyse this fat-headed trait of civilisation, but hidden in my overall view that many of these are designed to provide only good news (to those who otherwise might not get any), is my secondary opinion that these are useful feedback for a speaker – but not especially so. If your audiences are asked to fill one in, however, I would make it your business to get hold of a summation of the results – even if one is not sent to you voluntarily.

Working closely with event organisers is a key to speaking success. For more on this subject, try IDEA 2: *Ask not what your clients can do for you.*

Try another idea...

I find there are three additional ways to get useful feedback on a speech:

- Mingle with the audience afterwards. You are not going to get much criticism to your face, but if you get your antennae out you can pick up signals from overheard bits of conversation. You will get more objective feedback if you pop in and talk to the production and/or sound teams (if they exist). Ask them if they have any technical points to make.
- Always, always, write to (or email) the organiser (or the person who invited you to speak) after the event. Primarily this is a thank-you note, but you should ask for any comments and/or feedback that they might have – either on behalf of the audience or specifically from their point of view. I've found this to be quite fertile ground, particularly if they feel they can hide behind the impersonality of a note or email.
- If you get booked through a speaking agency, make sure they are briefed to pass on any feedback which is sent to them. This is probably your best source of possible bad news – and probably your best source of any needed step-function development material.

'Ever since I could talk, I was ordered to listen.'
CAT STEVENS

Defining idea...

191

How did it go?

Q **After seeing several 'speech' feedback forms, I have designed one to give out after my own speeches. It involves a simple (five-point) multiple choice 'marking' on various aspects of my speech – content, knowledge of subject, entertainment value etc. Is this a reliable form of achieving feedback?**

A *Look, if you've gone to all that trouble, and you are prepared to dish these things out every time you have finished a speech and then digest the results, then good luck to you. You will get some useful stuff – but I stand by my suspicion of these things. I believe they are self-serving of the people who give them out. Ask naturally and then listen intently.*

Q **I get my wife to listen in on my rehearsals at home. Isn't this the best way to get feedback?**

A *I am not a fan of hounding your husband/wife/best friend to criticise you during rehearsals at home. With the best will in the world you cannot give of the real thing, in your front room, without a live audience. I am a fan, however, of asking someone to sit in on a live performance now and again and report back how the audience responded.*

44

Same time next year?

This is for those speakers who want to do more. For some people that may be because it is a profession. For others, it is rewarding in different ways.

For all of them, there is no better time than the immediate aftermath of a successful speech to secure further bookings.

With the echo of applause still vaguely audible, and the final images of a successful speaker still imprinted on the mind, a lot of people are happy immediately after a successful speech. The audience, the organisers and any technical staff all feel good about the speaker. If there is any potential future business with any of these people, the time to secure it is right there, right then. One day later, 90% of the momentum is gone.

This surprises many speakers, even some who have been around the block a few times. Surely, the post-coital period after a speech is the last time you would seek future business? I mean, you have just spoken to this audience – surely they won't want to hear you again anytime soon? And isn't the immediate period after a speech a good time to secure the success of this one by mingling and following up on any questions from the audience?

Here's an idea for you...

Never start a speech without a mini sales-lead kit on your person. In my case that only involves a few business cards and a small pad and pen. Immediately after a successful speech it is sometimes difficult to get back to your bag or briefcase to get hold of this stuff. Those who are most interested will hit you with questions and/or enquiries straight away – and these are the folk you want to follow up with. You will also have a very limited time to make your 'friendly' pitch to the technical people – their minds and/or bodies will rapidly be moving on to the next speaker and/or venue.

The last point is valid, but my idea is not mutually exclusive to making sure the existing day is marked down in the 'win' column. Essentially, speakers who want more bookings become salespeople, with the product being themselves. Like all good salespeople, they have noses for an opportunity that resemble (a quote from an old Lancashire friend of mine) a blind cobbler's thumb. It was partly by accident, and partly by working it out, that I discovered that the thirty minutes after a successful speech is the best time to get good sales leads.

Here's how it works:

■ Sure, the audience you have just spoken to may not want to hear from you again in the near future – but they, as individuals, usually go back to other lives. If they've just witnessed you go down well, and they have enjoyed being part of that experience, they may be already trawling their minds for opportunities to use you in those other lives – in events they organise or influence.

If you've seen a speaker live, as a member of an audience, you are far more confident about putting your own reputation on the line by using (or recommending) them

To be a bit more sophisticated about selling yourself, try IDEA 50, *Me and my airbrush*.

Try another idea...

elsewhere. I spoke to a supply chain convention in the US, and immediately after got a lead from their South African sister organisation. I did that speech in Cape Town, and immediately after that one got another lead from an audience member for an entirely different organisation in Johannesburg...

■ If there are technical/production people involved, always find them afterwards and thank them. It does no harm to inject them with the idea that your success was entirely down to their professionalism. Take an interest in what they do, and if it transpires that this is what they do for a living (i.e. move from meeting to meeting, event to event), make sure they have your contact details. You would be surprised as to how many times event organisers first fix a date, then book a location, then recruit a production company and then ask the latter for recommendations on speakers.

■ If you've gone down well, the event organiser is sharing your success. They like that. It may well be that the organiser has responsibilities for organising other events, maybe within the same organisation, maybe elsewhere – so using you again becomes a (very) low-risk way of making themselves look good again. Now, how many of those opportunities come by in a year? You'd almost be selfish not to offer them the chance...

'Carpe diem. Quam minimum credula postero.'
(Seize the day; put no trust in tomorrow.)
HORACE

Defining idea...

195

Q **If you have a speaking agency representing you, isn't it unethical to go about getting bookings yourself?**

A *I'm not talking about doing this instead of your agent's efforts, I'm talking about doing this in addition to what they do. I'm not talking about closing a sale, I'm talking about opening a sales lead. It really is a unique opportunity, and, unless you are one of the really big guns, your agent will not be there. It's about identifying a possible future opportunity, getting whatever traction you can right there, right then – and then passing it to your agent to try and close the deal. Believe me, no agency on earth will be unhappy at that process.*

Q **I always write to an organiser after a speech I've given. That's primarily to say thank you – but isn't that the best time and process to seek any follow-up business?**

A *I still believe the initial sound-out is best done immediately after the speech, person to person. The next day, back in different locations, with the buzz of the speech just a memory, and just looking at a fax or an email, much of the impetus and momentum will have gone. Sadly, in my case, that usually applies to me as well.*

45

You at the back. Yes, you...

Many speaking invitations include a question and answer session at the end. If I get one, I see one of my first tasks as trying to talk the organisers out of it.

My experience tells me that these sessions are high-risk, low-reward interludes for everybody involved.

Ending a speech successfully and then hosting an open question and answer session is like winning the gold medal in the 100 metres and then wandering over to the high jump to try your luck. I'm not advocating that you stop communicating with the audience after a speech. Nor am I suggesting that it is wrong to leave any questions unanswered. The latter is impossible, and many of my speeches are deliberately designed to raise a lot of questions. I am saying that an open Q and A session, immediately after a speech, is not the best time or way to do it.

Here are three reasons why I dislike these:
- Organisers rarely get the technology right. Obviously the challenge is tougher as the audience gets bigger, but unless you've got a really good and portable sound system it becomes really frustrating for audiences over 100. Everybody is straining to hear and/or somebody is climbing over somebody else to get at a microphone.

Here's an idea for you... If you are not already doing so, stand up where you are now. Walk around pointing at objects, saying what they are. Then, after a few minutes of this, continue the walking and pointing, but say the names of the previous object you pointed at when you point at a new one. It gets your mouth used to saying one thing while your mind is on another. They use this technique to train for comedy 'impro' and it's great practice for Q and A.

- As a speaker, you've just finished – hopefully on a high note and to a nice response. For the duration of the speech you have been in control of the script and concentrating. Now, you're relaxed and not in control. That's a pretty sound formula for any speaker to 'say something stoopid'.

- An open forum hands the floor to anybody – a group that includes two species that you don't want near a microphone. The first are the 'Ramblers' – who go on for minutes without even vaguely coming to the point. The second are the 'Pricks' – (these are usually guys) who have their own agenda for the event and take the opportunity to voice it – thinly disguised as a question to an uninvolved and innocent guest speaker.

How do you handle any questions that the audience may have? My preferred process is to agree with the organiser and/or MC that they announce two things before you start. First: politely ask the audience not to raise questions during the speech. Second: say you will stay on after the speech and make yourself available for anybody who has questions – or, indeed, challenges or other ideas. In that way, those who are interested will get what they want without detaining the rest of the audience – and those who are intimidated by the idea of standing up in public don't have to miss out.

If, however, the organisers remain steadfast, and insist on questions and answers, here are some ideas for minimising the risk:

- If it's a big audience, insist that the technology is right – that the microphones can reach everybody.

Confidence is an important ingredient for handling Q and A. Try IDEA 28, *You're so vain*, for more thoughts on that subject.

Try another idea...

- If you do start a Q and A session, it is likely that the first experience will be a deafening silence. Nobody likes being first, so have a couple of rhetorical questions handy to ask yourself out loud (e.g. 'A lot of people ask me...' or 'Perhaps you are wondering...').

- When a question has been asked, repeat it out loud, over your microphone. This does two things: it makes sure you (and the audience) have heard it correctly, and it gives you a bit of time to think about your answer.

- Take every question seriously. You are relaxed, and there's a temptation to swat away what you think are silly questions. If you've won over your audience during your speech, this is a good way to lose them.

- Get on familiar ground as soon as possible. You've probably got a lot of material that you haven't used in your particular speech on that day. If it's possible, work the question/answer back to that – it's so much better to respond with stuff that's familiar to you.

- Don't bluff. If you don't know, say so. You can score more points by then proposing you get back with the answer. Perhaps you could suggest those interested should pass their email addresses to the organiser so that you can do so.

'If you open that Pandora's box, you never know what Trojan horses will jump out.'
ERNEST BEVIN, British politician

Defining idea...

201

How did it go?

Q   **In a recent Q and A session, an audience member had a real go at me. I'm not sure whether it was me or somebody else who had upset him, but it felt unfair and I was annoyed. Was I right to respond aggressively?**

A   *You can't win by doing that – the audience will switch from you to him in a heartbeat. If somebody does get aggressive and/or personal, I would stay polite, agree to disagree, throw a verbal fire blanket on him quickly and move on.*

Q   **Is it OK to use a couple of 'planted' questions in a Q and A session?**

A   *Yes. It's another way of breaking the 'deafening silence' that usually starts one. The organiser and/or the MC are good vehicles for this – if they've agreed a Q and A session, suggest to them that they lead in with a question if it's quiet. If necessary, leave a couple of 'friendly' questions with them.*

46

Here's one I prepared earlier

Handouts provided by a speaker are an exercise in the unwilling providing the unwanted to the uninterested.

On the rare occasions they are appropriate, take them seriously and use software technology to make the whole process better, cheaper and easier.

I decided to shock you by calculating how many presentations/speeches, etc., I have 'received' in my lifetime. I gave up counting. I then calculated how many handouts I might have received with these speeches, and I figure that to be between 5 and 10% of whatever the first figure was. I then calculated how many of these handouts I actually wanted, and how many I actually read when I got back home. No inaccuracy or guesswork here: the two answers are zero and zero, respectively.

Now, you just might be an educational lecturer who cannot envisage a presentation unaccompanied by lecture summaries and/or lists of further reading and/or references. However, for the most part a speech is a finite event and the whole thing finishes, for all parties, with the applause. There may be some needs on both sides to follow up on some things, but in my view – if you have done your job as a speaker properly – these will only involve a few members of the audience and/or a

Reduce your speech's sections/key points into two- or three-sentence summaries. Import them into text boxes in a new DTP document. Arrange the boxes to reflect the sequence in which they occur in your speech. Then position two new boxes – one at the top and one at the bottom of the page. In the top one, put the client's name and the date and location of the event; in the bottom one put your own name and contact details. You then have the blueprint for a handout – which you can change easily (for example, with new sections, new client details, etc.).

few elements that justify additional attention. I can only think of two sets of circumstances where a handout, which includes a reprise of the speech itself, is warranted:

■ Where the client wants – nay, insists – on it. This is not uncommon, and innocent enough. Organisers sometimes want delegates to have a record of the event, and will ask a speaker for a summary in suitable format so that it can be included. In these cases the customer is always right, so grin and bear it.

■ If you do need to refer to a lot of information and/or data in your speech, it may actually improve your performance if you choose not to clutter your oratory up with numerous slides or verbal references. In these cases you may wish to cherry-pick the key facts for your speech, and include the more peripheral stuff in a handout.

My big concern about handouts is not down to laziness (honest!), but because they restrict the flexibility of a speaker. By definition, if you are going to provide handouts that include the key points of your speech, you are going to have to have them done and dusted before you start. This leaves you committed to deliver the planned contents – and it is my belief that good speakers should retain the right to change content, order and emphasis once they have got a 'feel' for the audience.

If you do have to do it, here are some ideas on making handouts painless.

- Do not give the thing out before (or during) your speech. Apart from the distraction of having an audience shuffle paper while you are speaking, it dilutes your impact enormously if your audience has even a summary of your content and structure beforehand.

- Keep it as brief as possible. Brutally summarise each of your speech sections/key points into two or three sentences in a way that when (if?) they are read, they will trigger a memory of you making the fuller point. If you are giving a list of sources and/or further reading and/or references try and keep the whole thing to a single page.

- Technology has made this kind of thing so much easier. If you can use DTP (desktop publishing) software then you can reduce what was a burdensome task for a previous generation of speakers into a very quick, client-specific and professional document-producing exercise in half an hour or so. Again, I would stress, limit your handout to one sheet, and limit the verbiage to summaries of the key points. Get your impact through colour and font variety.

For more thoughts on structuring your speech into finite sections, see IDEA 14: One step at a time.

Try another idea…

'Thanks for the memory.'
LEO RUBIN, songwriter

Defining idea…

'Don't mention it, Leo. It's just a memento of my speech. I hope you enjoy reading it as much as I enjoyed putting it together.'
BARRY GIBBONS

…and another…

How did it go?

Q **I use a lot of slides, and bring (paper) copies of them with me just in case the projector breaks down and I have to improvise. Wouldn't it make sense to expand this practice and give audience members hard copies of my slides afterwards?**

A *As a backup, your idea makes a lot of sense. As a handout, it's a nightmare. If a speaker presented me with a wad of paper after a speech, which consisted of copies of a load of slides without the context of the accompanying speech, I would downgrade my view of both the speaker and the speech. If you are going to give a handout, design it properly.*

Q **Isn't giving a handout a good opportunity to get your contact name and details 'out there' for future speaking opportunities?**

A *I'm all for selling yourself as a speaker, and all for using the immediate aftermath of a speech to do so. I just don't think a handout is the best vehicle for doing it – and, indeed, may inhibit you from taking advantage of a potentially positive repeat-business climate by focusing conversation on the past, and not on future opportunities.*

47

Team A will be on the sofa by the fire doors

It may be that your first or most frequent occasion to speak in public is not via a solo spot – but as part of a group exercise.

Your success criteria and occasion dynamics change profoundly.

Speaking solo, when it comes to what you want to achieve with your speech, you can aim as high as you want to. Quite simply, the only limitations are your (self-defined) powers of persuasion and perceived credibility. If you are involved with a group – either as a leader or a member – your goals as a speaker must reflect more of the potential inhibitions rather than the potential synergy. Experience has taught me a golden rule: underpromise and overdeliver.

Although every group session is different, some ideas can be common to them all, because whatever they're called – workshops, seminars, break-outs, etc. – they are a modern organisational pandemic. If an audience has just had a presentation (which could be your speech) there is a perceived need not to let it stop there. With increasing frequency, the organisers want the information receivers to digest it and then contribute themselves – for example, with how what they've heard could be

Review an imminent or recent speech of yours and – on one page – structure a brief for a workshop session based on it. Take your most powerful idea/position/proposal – then leave your defined groups to develop ideas as to how they would adapt and implement it, how they would define the success criteria and so on. Think through what your role would be in facilitating this, how long would be needed, and what the feedback logistics and overall process would be. Then, the next time somebody questions whether you could do it, answer 'yes' with confidence.

applied to their lives. Even without a speaker, it is common now for organisations to try and institutionalise their listening skills (otherwise known as 'delegation', 'empowerment', 'participation' and 'input' processes, etc.) by getting groups together to chew things over and put forward ideas. All variations can involve public speaking.

Whether you lead or are a member of the pack, you will do well to remember that these fields are mined with frustration. When you fly solo as a speaker, you are in control of your output. You are in control of your position, and the reasoning behind it. You are in control of your sequence, content and timing. If you are uncomfortable with anything, you can stick the telescope to your blind eye. You need seek no consensus. All those change when a group is involved.

If a task is set, and a time defined for it, there is an assumption that if you put more human resources into it, then more will get done, much better and more quickly. That is wrong. The opposite occurs. There are many, many reasons why, so just accept it for now – and bear in mind the implications for a speaker/participant. It may be that you are a speaker who has been asked to chair a follow-up 'workshop', in which case you can control the group's effectiveness and efficiency. It may be that you are just a group member – in which case you will need to be Machiavellian to influence the same things. Either way, factor into the process my thesis that the only time I have seen

> **If you are leading, or trying to be assertive in a group, it's handy to be good with a chart pad. Look up IDEA 25, *Can you tell what it is yet?***

Try another idea…

anything effective come out of a workshop is where it set about a limited task and went on to overachieve it.

Here's how you can control or influence the process to reach these depths. Let's say you have given a speech, and you have agreed to chair a workshop on how the organisation might encompass some of your ideas. Don't go for a multidimensional set of proposals, even if that's what you've suggested and that's what you believe is needed. Go for one idea. In other words get the group to identify and agree on one thing that could work for them. Then, instead of getting them to list fifteen more, get them to use their energy on pounding the one idea – to make sure it's thought through and that it's robust. Then stay on the one idea – and get them to identify in advance how they will know if it's been implemented successfully. If there's any time left, then figure out, collectively, how they might review its future progress.

If you are not leading the group, use your assertiveness within it to get as near as you can to this formula. In this way, there is a chance that the group will come up with a jewel of an idea which is useable – i.e. realistically capable of implementation. The alternative is usually a laundry list of undercooked bollocks.

> **'Aim low. Reach your goals. Avoid disappointment.'**
> Spoof office inspirational poster

Defining idea…

209

How did it go?

Q **I am organising some workshop sessions after my next speech. I have an audience of fifty that needs breaking up into groups. What's the best number per group?**

A *I find the lower the (individual) group membership the more useable the output, but that is not the only criterion that needs to be taken into account. You need to make sure that each group has an adequate location and proper facilities, and you need to factor in the logistics of reporting back. Probably seven or eight per group will work for you – but, whatever the occasion, it should never be more than ten.*

Q **If you have the job of reporting back on behalf of a group, how much 'poetic licence' can you employ to shape the group's position into your own?**

A *You will have less if the group follows my idea of concentrating on one thing and thinking it right through. In general, there are many trade-offs to make if you accept or coerce the position of leader of the group. Be careful though – few 'personal gains' are worth pissing off your peer group for.*

48

Ich bin ein Berliner

There is a possibility that, as your prowess and reputation as a speaker grows, you will be asked to address an audience whose primary language is not your own.

What fun...

When addressing an audience in what is for them a second language, or through an interpreter, you must forget your normal modus operandi. Of all the new things you must remember, the key one is that your mind must reprogramme your mouth. You must speak as though your vocal chords are constipated.

There are, broadly, two types of challenge in the field of 'foreign' public speaking. First, your audience will not understand English – in which case you will have to speak through a (simultaneous) translator. In some cases, such an audience may have a number of nationalities present, so the simultaneous translation could be into as many as five or six languages. In all these instances, the translation is fed to the listener via headphones, and the 'simultaneous' bit is misleading because there is a lag between your spoken words and the listener receiving the translated version – which may be as much as twenty seconds. The second type of challenge is where you will work without a translator, but the language you speak is the second language of the audience. They sound very different for a speaker, but they are not.

Here's an idea for you... **If you have been invited to give a speech to an international audience, or there is a likelihood of that happening, take your normal speech and do two things to it. First, simplify your language dramatically and then treat the residue as though it was to be fed to you via Autocue – with the varying pauses clearly annotated. This will give you a good base to then make the appropriate cultural adjustments.**

Here are some ideas whereby you can avoid creating a diplomatic incident.

■ I am not, in the normal course of events, one for leaving too much on the practice ground. I am one for a speaker having faith in him or herself and retaining the flexibility to wing it. This does not apply on these occasions. Preparation is everything here. You need to prepare your speech almost to the word – because every word or phrase needs careful overhaul to ensure it contains no unknown (to you) mistakes or offences.

■ Pacing is everything. Whether you are doing it via an interpreter or to an audience in their second language, you need to slow it down. Dramatically. One idea (I use) is to try and speak as Hemingway advocated you should write – short sentences, short paragraphs, no adverbs. That's easier for the translator and an audience not overly familiar with your language, particularly if you allow long pauses after each full stop. This has big implications for your own timing. If you are asked, for example, to do a thirty-minute speech, reduce your normal material by a third.

- Remember the 'HSBC factor'. This international bank has a global advertising campaign built around the fact that a friendly or common gesture in one part of the world can be gratuitously offensive in another. I quote this for two reasons. First, it is very sound advice, and you need to make yourself aware of any local cultural dos and don'ts before you go. Second, it allows me to mention the Hongkong and Shanghai Bank's (HSBC) nickname – which is the best I have ever heard. It is the Honkers and Shaggers.

- Pay some homage to the locality you are visiting. This is not likely to be an overnight call, so spend some time beforehand familiarising yourself with what's going on in the place. What are the big political, social and sports stories? Who are the key movers and shakers? You may be able to adapt some of your own stories or substitute examples accordingly.

- Humour doesn't travel well. This unfortunate fact applies to both content and style, so your hilarious anecdote that, without fail, has your home audiences slapping their thighs and crying tears of joy probably needs ditching. This factor also applies between the US and the UK. It hurts me to say this, but you should rake out all but the shortest, cleanest and clearest funny stuff and just get the job done.

Imagining you are using Autocue is a very helpful way of preparing a speech for an international audience. For more information on this, try IDEA 33: *I seem to have moved from 33 to 45 rpm.*

Try another idea...

'Ich bin ein Berliner.'
JOHN F. KENNEDY, in Berlin during the Cold War – he meant to imply that he was a spiritual Berliner, but his remarks can also be translated as him saying that he was a cake...

Defining idea...

How did it go?

Q **I am English and have been invited to give a speech to a French audience. Should I get my speech translated into French and do it in their own language?**

A *Unless you are fluent in French for both translation and delivery, this seems like a lot of effort to go to, just to create more potential risk than reward. It might work if you are giving a short toast or introduction, but for a speech of any length, to any 'foreign' audience, I would suggest you stay in your own 'natural' language and adapt the style and content in the ways I have mentioned above. It is for the event organisers to determine if formal translation is needed.*

Q **If you are speaking through a translator, should you wait until each bit has been translated before moving on to the next? Or should you just accept your speech will be 'lagged' in its delivery to the listener – and get on with it?**

A *As most simultaneous translations are now fed to the listener by earphone, you won't know the exact moment when they receive the final word of your previous bit. This situation can be made more complex if your speech is being translated into more than one language – in which case it will arrive at different times within the same audience. The best advice I can give is follow the style and content rules, and get on with it.*

överga...

transit-trade [træ'nsittreid, tr
transitohandel
Transjordania [træ'nzdʒɔ:dei'n
Transjordanien
translat‖able [trɑ:nslei'|təbl, t
översättlig -e [-t] I *tr* **1** över|sä
[*into* till, *by* med visst ord]; ~d
översatt (i översättning) från
engelska originalet); *kindly*
uttryck dig (er) tydligare **2**
tyda;, uppfatta [*this* I ~d *as*
flytta isht biskop till annat stift
helgedom **4** bibl. upptaga ngn [
melen; hädankalla **5** förändr
till]; ~ *into action* omsätta i
m. m. överföra, vidarebo

49

Thieving magpies

Most speakers collect silly bits and pieces of information and prose. They don't have a collective name for them, and they don't really know why they do it...

They just know these things come in useful at various times in a speech.

I'm a bit more scientific. I call them 'ells'. That is because the roles they perform in a speech generally begin with the letter 'L' – i.e. Looseners, Left-fielders, Lighteners and Links.

The collection of ells is not plagiarism. Plagiarism is stealing material from one source. Stealing from many sources (aka the science of ellogy) is called research. By this definition, speakers are profound researchers – rather like magpies.

Ells are not one-liners – although they are generally short and pithy. If an audience is a bit uptight, they loosen it up. If it is overfocused, they make everybody think sideways. If it's a bit gloomy (or sleepy) they brighten it up. If you (the speaker) need to pause and regroup, they link sections by making an audience think and smile while you sip your water and get ready for the next bit. There is no way to define these things beforehand, so you can't go out ell-hunting. But every speaker

217

Here's an idea for you…

Start today and collect numeric ells. Use an old notebook, or dump them in a PC file. Tell you what, here are the first couple to start you off. 1: The Great Pyramid of Cheops in Egypt was 147 m high – exactly one billionth of the distance between the earth and sun. 2: There are twice as many plastic flamingos in the US as there are real ones. Now over to you: 3? Keep collecting – ad infinitum. You'll find a use for them one day. Here's number 41: 'The average bed has more than forty-one hundred million dust mites…'

knows one when they see it. To save you a lot of trouble, here are a bunch that have worked for me:

- What's the shortest verse in the Bible? I had no idea either until I saw it written in some other context somewhere. It consists of two words: Jesus wept. You can use this in a bunch of different ways without offence. (My suggestion is that Jesus was on the phone to his bank's call centre, and had just been put on hold again…)
- Bits of bogus philosophy make great ells, such as 'you can never underestimate the power of very stupid people in large groups'.
- Indecision is the key to flexibility.
- OK. So – what's the speed of dark?
- I like reading obituaries. Isn't it amazing how all those people die in alphabetical order?
- I always put a dab of perfume on my income tax return. If they are doing that to me, I should at least smell nice.
- Some universal laws make good ells: 'Prudhomme's Law of Window Cleaning states: it is always on the other side.'
- As a male, your life is effectively over on the day you put aside a piece of thin wood specifically to stir paint with.
- Beethoven was so deaf that he thought he was a painter.

- The male gypsy moth can smell the virgin gypsy moth from 1.8 miles away (but does he ever call? Noooo…).
- What's unique about this sentence: 'A rough-coated, dough-faced, thoughtful ploughman strode through the streets of Slough: after falling into a slough, he coughed and hiccoughed'? It contains the many different ways of pronouncing 'ough' in the English language.
- Emus and kangaroos cannot walk backwards – which is the reason they are on the Australian flag.
- A shin is a device for finding furniture in the dark.
- What happens if you get scared half to death – twice?
- The hardness of the butter is mathematically correlated to the softness of the bread.
- The word 'testify' was based on men in the Roman court swearing to a statement by swearing on the testicles. Now think about O.J. Simpson…
- The first ever episode of 'Joanie loves Chachi' was the highest ever rated American TV program in the history of Korean television. You would not believe what *chachi* is in Korean…
- Some days you are a pigeon. Some days you are a statue.

Using ells normally involves humour. For more thoughts on what you can, and can't, get away with, try IDEA 16, *Laugh? I thought I'd never start.*

Try another idea…

'I nick, therefore I speak.'
DÉSCARTES (in his later years, as an after-dinner speaker)

Defining idea…

Q **If you openly steal a humorous line from somebody, shouldn't you acknowledge the source in your speech?**

A *This is all down to a matter of degree. How recent and/or famous is the line? If it was on nationwide TV the night before, then you would be foolish to put it out as your own. If your speech is high profile, then you increase the risk of somebody catching you out. If in doubt, mention the source – you won't use many of these in a speech and it's not a big deal. There is a line by Billy Connolly that I use: 'There's no such thing as bad weather, there's only the wrong clothes'. It is a delightful ell for all sorts of audiences – it's actually quite profound as well as daft. If I use it, I preface it by acknowledging the source.*

Q **If there's a bit of philosophy and fun combined, isn't that a good mix to finish on – almost guaranteeing a laugh and applause – so is it a good tactic to end a speech with one of these lines?**

A *It is a very popular way to end a speech – but your closing is your most memorable part so it needs to be just right for you. I can't pick this for you – but if you keep looking you will know the right one when you see it. Meanwhile, I would like to end this piece with some advice. Never, never end a piece with advice.*

50

Me and my airbrush

As a speaker who wants to do more speaking, you are selling a product in a cluttered competitive market. That product is you.

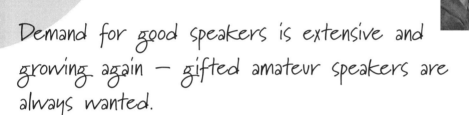

Demand for good speakers is extensive and growing again — gifted amateur speakers are always wanted.

The market for professional speakers, however, tends to correlate with the economic climate – and that looks to be coming out of the dark times at the turn of the millennium. That's the end of the good news because, although demand is growing, the supply of gifted speakers is keeping pace with it.

The selling of you requires you to market yourself effectively and efficiently. To market yourself in this way requires you to blow your own trumpet. It is not a game normally won by the falsely modest; it is not an earth that will be inherited by the meek.

A lot of people are uncomfortable with selling themselves, but it is really no different from the marketing and selling of any product. In the latter you always concentrate on the positive and add a bit of poetic licence. In selling yourself, you just substitute vanity for bullshit. So here are some ideas on selling yourself as a speaker.

Here's an idea for you...

Think of yourself as a branded product or service. If a brand is going to succeed in cluttered, competitive markets it needs to be distinct. It may seem basic, but you need to be able to understand why you, as a speaker, are distinct – and to be able to articulate that. Now, here's the tricky bit – most great brands can do that in a few words. You should be able to crayon it on the back of a business card. It sounds simple, but may take a long time to get it right – so start now.

I have found that, even in the age of the internet, a very helpful sales and marketing aid is a double-sided, three-panel brochure. You can mail it and/or use it as a business card – but it gets a hard-copy, hard-selling, purpose-built document in the hands of decision makers. You can also use this as a basis of your own website. I have had my brochure produced professionally; you might be capable of using desk-top publishing to do it yourself. Where it's done doesn't matter – but it must 'signal' quality and professionalism as decisions will be made on it. Here's how I structure the six panels on my brochure:

- *Front panel*: Name, photograph and one line describing why I am distinct. Get your photograph done professionally, and get it capable of being emailed. I can't stress this enough, even if it does sound vain and overexpensive. A picture is worth a thousand words in selling, and a head and shoulders photo of you taken by your teenage daughter with her 3G mobile phone will not do.
- *Second panel:* On mine this answers the questions 'who is he?' (summary biography) and 'where is he?' (where I'm based and where I travel).
- *Third panel:* This also answers questions – 'what do audiences learn?' (my core subjects); 'what doesn't the audience learn?' (a bit of fun, e.g. how many ceiling tiles there are in the room, the number of people wearing blue shirts, etc.); and 'how does he do it?' (typical speech length, position on Q and A, workout sessions, etc.).

- *Fourth Panel:* Answers the question 'does it work?' (mine simply lists quoted endorsements from clients).
- *Fifth Panel:* A selected list of clients and another, smaller, photograph.
- *Sixth (back) panel:* Contact details.

You should also have a flexible one-page summary of your biography and sales pitch, which contains a head-and-shoulders photograph, as a PC file. You should be able to email this, proactively or reactively, to anybody, and be able to adapt its contents to suit the purpose (e.g. if an enquiry comes through an agent, then include the information that you are represented by them). Keep this right up to date.

Finally, don't forget the power of the technical people – professional conference organisers, production companies, etc. – when you are 'leaving your calling card'. If you have performed well at a successful conference that has involved these kinds of professionals, they will be happy to repeat the formula with other clients if they get the chance. This might include recommending speakers – so make sure they've got several copies of your sales brochure to help them.

Marketing and selling yourself is all about confidence. For more ideas on making yourself sure-footed, try IDEA 28, *You're so vain.*

Try another idea…

'Vanity of vanities; all is vanity.'
The Bible

Defining idea…

223

How did
it go?

**Q   I noticed at a recent speech I gave that the client was recording it
on video. Should I insist on a copy?**

A   *The first point to make is that this shouldn't be a surprise – you should not
be recorded on video without agreeing it beforehand. However, if a video
recording has been made of your speech, and it has gone well, beg,
borrow, steal or kill to get a copy. Get it transferred onto DVD and/or CD-
ROM, and you have a powerful sales tool at your disposal.*

**Q   If I use agents to represent me in the speaking market, isn't it
counter-productive to develop my own sales and marketing
support aids?**

A   *If you work through agents there are two things to remember. First, there is
a difference between a sales 'lead' and closing the deal. The agent will
want to sign the contract, and you should want them to do all that stuff –
but the agent doesn't really care where the original lead comes from.
Secondly, and linked to the first point, you will have many opportunities
(including on the day of a speech) where you can open a new sales lead via
an opportunity that is not available to an agent. What does make sense is
to leave the back panel of your brochure (i.e. contact information) blank,
and have some stickers printed for different follow-up contacts.*

51

I'm obviously earning 20% too much

If you are really serious about speaking in public, you will need an agent to get you more speeches and to represent your contractual interests.

When it comes to reaching out to the market, and making the right deals, the resources and reach of a specialist agent are essential.

You can succeed on your own in the speaking market – but only to a degree. You can land the opportunities that present themselves to you. A good agent is not just about the marketing and selling of 'you'. It is about finding the right clients and then doing the right deal. Unfortunately, the handshake has disappeared from western civilisation as a way of agreeing a contract, and the legal aspects of a simple speech appearance today are such that you can either bog yourself down or get help. The latter is a big part of a good agent's role.

If you are not a big name, it is difficult to get an agent from a cold start. In short, you need to sell them the idea that you will make them money – which is different from selling to an audience the fact you are a good speaker. If you don't have an agent, design yourself a one-page sales brief for a potential agent, built around the premise that 'this is how you will make money out of me'.

I have been fortunate in that the first agency who represented me, over a decade ago, in the US, was a role model not only for this specialist business – but for all service businesses. The Washington Speakers Bureau, run by Harry Rhoads, Bernie Swain (and ably assisted by Tony D'Amelio) is still (exclusively) looking after my US speaking activities. It is much bigger nowadays, but you wouldn't know it from the personal service they give. I have other agents, on a non-exclusive basis, elsewhere in the world, but what my relationship with WSB has enabled me to do is define the best model for a speaker/agent relationship. Here it is:

- However big the agency, and however small you are in their portfolio, if they don't come and watch you speak very early on in your relationship, they are not for you. They can have all the videos, endorsements and sales aids in the world – but unless somebody has seen you perform they can't represent you properly. If they are not interested enough to invest that time, they are not the right choice.
- Don't haggle with the agency fee (usually a percentage). If anything, insist they increase it. You want these folk to be incentivised to get you more business. If they land you one more speech through their extra enthusiasm, this 'investment' (by you in them) more than pays back.
- Give them the tools to do the job. You will be one of the 'products' they sell and, as such, will be listed in their catalogue or (more likely nowadays) on their

website. Their website functions as do all websites – crap in equals crap out. So make sure you take the initiative and provide them with up-to-date quality stuff about yourself and your activities. Remember, when a potential client scrolls through the list of speakers provided by an agency, you are in direct competition with the other speakers. With this in mind, it's worth checking your competition out now and again.

For more specific thoughts on selling yourself, try IDEA 50, *Me and my airbrush*.

Try another idea...

- If you have a lead for a possible speech, make sure your potential client knows you will be doing the final negotiation and contract through an agent. Then get it into that process (i.e. between them) as soon as possible.
- Conversely, if an agent has a lead, and seems to be having difficulty in closing the deal, then be prepared to help out. It may be that the client seeks an exploratory chat with you before committing – so make sure your agent knows that you are prepared to help, within reason.
- Once the contract is signed, my experience is that an agent is not good at getting you briefed and sorting out logistics. They may feel they are, or feel they should – but my belief is that these details are best sorted out directly between you and the client.
- An agency has a different relationship with the client than you do. It may be that they get stuff fed back to them – which can range from copies of videos, endorsement letters or formal feedback data on your performance by audiences. You can use all of this, either to enhance your selling materials or simply to learn, so make sure there is a process in place for your agent to get this stuff to you.

'An oral contract is not worth the paper it's written on.'
SAMUEL GOLDWYN

Defining idea...

227

How did it go?

Q   **I do not have an exclusive agency, and was recently approached by two agencies for the same speech. How do I respond?**

A   *A client will sometimes ask a production company for a 'full package' for an event, and the production company will then go out to different speaking agencies to quote for the same event. Your name can come up twice. It's embarrassing, but if you haven't got an exclusive or a favourite agent, just be honest with both agencies and tell them to sort it out. It's their problem, not yours.*

Q   **If I tie myself exclusively to one agent, are there likely to be more downsides for me than benefits?**

A   *By definition, the answer is unquantifiable. Obviously, all agents would like exclusive representation rights for their speakers, but the volume of business has to justify it. You do not have to lose out on all other agency business, however, as some agencies will subcontract or split the fee if a client specifically requests a speaker from another agent.*

52

These guys are good

No speaker should fail today because of lack of advice, or guidance, on the subject...

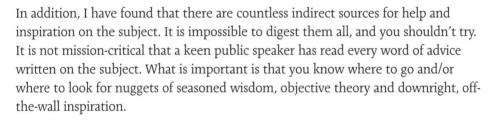

If you go into one of the modern 'mega bookstores', you will find substantial acreage (and probably a small coffee bar) dedicated to the topic of speaking in public.

In addition, I have found that there are countless indirect sources for help and inspiration on the subject. It is impossible to digest them all, and you shouldn't try. It is not mission-critical that a keen public speaker has read every word of advice written on the subject. What is important is that you know where to go and/or where to look for nuggets of seasoned wisdom, objective theory and downright, off-the-wall inspiration.

I read a lot (*a lot*) of books about speaking during my first couple of years as a professional speaker, but then I gave up. I trawled another gaggle of them recently, but they just confirmed my earlier views. Bits and pieces, here and there, were helpful, but no single speaking guru could provide a model that kept working for me as I changed, audiences changed and technology changed.

Here's an idea for you…

DVDs have enabled a lot of influencing and learning material to become available to you in your own home. Go and buy four – two American and two UK stand-up comedians – and see what you can pick up. See how Robin Williams screams at the audience, whereas Jerry Seinfeld embraces them. It's almost as though Jerry is in there with the audience, and they are all addressing somebody else. These are two entirely different techniques – which suits you best? Then look at the UK's Ricky Gervais, and his clever use of a lectern as an anchor point – it's where he goes for water (or a beer!), a glance at his notes or a mental re-group. Then look at Eddie Izzard, who never tells a joke, but makes ordinary life hilarious by exaggerating, just a little, the ordinary things we witness. Peter Kay does a northern UK version of this. When you've done these, you are up and running – start your own collection with your own speaking style in mind.

There simply isn't one book which I could recommend that I could be sure would provide you with all the answers you need. The nearest one – in my view – is *Just Say a Few Words* by Bob Monkhouse, the British comedian. It is a gem of sound practical and theoretical advice, and there's a load of stuff you can use. Do try and find it, and if you do get hold of one (it has been reissued but might disappear again), treasure it.

Here are some others that are useful for bits.

- *The Oxford Union Guide to Speaking in Public* (Dr Dominic Hughes and Benedict Phillips; Virgin Books).
- *Perfect Presentation* (Andrew Leigh and Michael Maynard; Random House).
- *Effective Presentation* (Ros Jay and Anthony Jay; Pearson Education).
- *Speaking Your Mind* (Rebecca Scott, Tony Young, Cordelia Bryan; Pearson Education). This is excellent on the complex subject of rhetoric.
- *Handbook for the Terrified Speaker* (Mitch Murray; Foulsham).
- *Speaking in Public* (Collins Pocket Reference).

- *How to Develop Self-confidence and Influence People by Public Speaking* (Dale Carnegie; Vermillion). This is a modern edition of the 1957 classic.
- *Penguin Book of Historic Speeches* (Penguin Books). A great one for the bedside. You won't get much source material you can use, but you will get a feel for good structure, rhetoric, impact and figurative language.

For some more information on references, research and role models, try IDEA 36, *As I am sure you will have read in* The Economist.

Try another idea...

Finally, it was Tom Peters who introduced me to the idea that inspiration can cross-fertilise. I was listening to a business seminar of his, and he advised (well, yelled) that we shouldn't get guidance on how to manage well from management books – but that we should read novels. Management is about characters and relationships, and where better to find inspiration? I transferred this thinking to speaking, and found myself inspired by people like the old Irish newspaper columnists and writers (Patrick Campbell, Brendan Behan, Myles na Gopaleen), and being influenced in my speaking by their written language and alliteration. These may not work for you, but what will work is the idea that you open your mind. Think differently about anybody you see, hear or read: is there something about their style or content you can use?

'No good model ever accounted for all facts.'
JAMES DEWEY WATSON, US scientist and writer

Defining idea...

Q   I find I need to be a Jekyll and Hyde creature to speak well in public. I only succeed when I abandon my normal (rather reticent) way of thinking and speaking. Are there any good advice books on how to do this?

A   *Good speakers do tend to be larger than life – and you are right in that the content needs to be in line with the performance. I have two of Tom Peters'* books *(The Pursuit of WOW and the* Tom Peters Seminar *– both published by Vintage Original). A quick browse through either helps you to raise your combustion and bombast levels before you speak!*

Q   Is the web a practical source for more information on public speaking?

A   *The web is, of course, a wondrous source of information on anything and everything, and it is a source that only really became available ten to fifteen years ago. Type the words 'public speaking' into your search engine, and if it's Google you will get nearly four million hits. You will get access to sources on everything to do with speaking in public, from toasting to corporate presentations, from conquering fear to every speaking agency worth a toss. It's overwhelming, so know (or, at least, have a feel for) what you want before you go in. If you can narrow your search to the specific guidance area you are looking for, it can be a very practical way of getting help.*

233

The end...

Or is it a new beginning? We hope that the ideas in this book will have given you all the insights you need to get up there and wow your audience. You've got the stage presence of Laurence Olivier, the presentation skills of Steven Spielberg and the dynamism of Madonna so you know they're going to be impressed.

So why not let us know about it? Tell us how you got on. What did it for you – what won over the delegates at the double glazing sales conference or made your best man's speech go with a bang? Maybe you've got some tips of your own you want to share (see the next page if so). And if you liked this book you may find we have even more brilliant ideas that could change other areas of your life for the better.

You'll find the Infinite Ideas crew waiting for you online at www.infideas.com.

Or if you prefer to write, then send your letters to:
Speak easy
The Infinite Ideas Company Ltd
36 St Giles, Oxford OX1 3LD, United Kingdom

We want to know what you think, because we're all working on making our lives better too. Give us your feedback and you could win a copy of another *52 Brilliant Ideas* book of your choice. Or maybe get a crack at writing your own.

Good luck. Be brilliant.

Offer one

CASH IN YOUR IDEAS

We hope you enjoy this book. We hope it inspires, amuses, educates and entertains you. But we don't assume that you're a novice, or that this is the first book that you've bought on the subject. You've got ideas of your own. Maybe our author has missed an idea that you use successfully. If so, why not send it to yourauthormissedatrick@infideas.com, and if we like it we'll post it on our bulletin board. Better still, if your idea makes it into print we'll send you four books of your choice or the cash equivalent. You'll be fully credited so that everyone knows you've had another Brilliant Idea.

Offer two

HOW COULD YOU REFUSE?

Amazing discounts on bulk quantities of Infinite Ideas books are available to corporations, professional associations and other organisations.

For details call us on:
+44 (0)1865 514888
Fax: +44 (0)1865 514777
or e-mail: info@infideas.com

Where it's at...

Even more brilliant ideas...

Secrets of wine

Giles Kime

"Forget the wine snobbery, the 'bouquet reminiscent of elderberries drying on a nun's bicycle seat' approach; this pretentious imagery seems to dominate the world of wine and the wine bores who spout such expressions all have one thing in common. Their heads are full of other people's ideas. In Secrets of wine I offer an insider's guide to the real world of wine... the kind of advice that allows you to come up with your own thoughts. It's time for you to become a free-thinking drinker!"
Giles Kime

Available from all good bookshops or call us on + 44 (0) 1865 514888

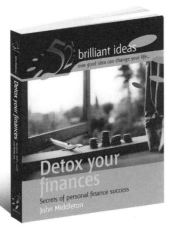

Detox your finances

John Middleton

"As an average citizen you'll probably spend at least one million pounds in the course of your working life. You're also likely to spend more than you earn, fail to realise your full earning potential and buy lots of stuff you don't really want or need. I know I did, but I decided to change. I had some ideas to get myself out of debt and financial denial and I put them into practice. Since then I've helped thousands of people sort out their own finances and now I can help you.

That's my story. This is yours. It starts here..." – **John Middleton**